The

WESTSIDE PARK MURDERS

The
WESTSIDE PARK
MURDERS

Muncie's Most Notorious Cold Case

Keith Roysdon and Douglas Walker

THE
History
PRESS

Published by The History Press
Charleston, SC
www.historypress.com

Front cover: Suspect sketch. *Authors' collection.* Crime scene photograph. *Courtesy of Muncie Newspapers.* Photograph of Ethan Dixon and Kimberly Dowell. *Courtesy of Anthony Dowell.* Westside Park at night, 2019. *Photograph by Jordan Kartholl.*

First published 2021

Manufactured in the United States

ISBN 9781467144889

Library of Congress Control Number: 2020945864

CONTENTS

INTRODUCTION

The murders of Ethan Dixon and Kimberly Dowell shook their hometown of Muncie, Indiana, which was once touted as "America's Hometown," to its core. In September 1985, the two teenagers—the offspring of Muncie doctors and industrialists and students at a privileged high school on the rich side of the tracks—were shot to death in Westside Park, a rambling green space along White River on the city's west side.

Muncie, a city of seventy-six thousand people less than an hour northeast of Indianapolis, had been cited in sociological studies as the typical small American city. But Muncie was no stranger to murder and shocking, unexplained deaths. The city, divided by railroad tracks into communities of affluent families and blue-collar workers, was a town that was, at times, marked by violence. Much of it was unexplained and unanswered; dozens of unsolved cold case homicides remained on the books decades after the lives of the victims had been snuffed out.

The Westside Park slayings of Dixon and Dowell stood apart because they seemed so unexpected, so surprising. Dixon, who was sixteen at the time, was a member of the debate team at Northside High School, an institution of learning that had its own divisive history. Dowell, fifteen at the time, was a junior varsity cheerleader for the school. They weren't known as kids who could have been involved in activities that would bring them into the sights of a killer's gun.

Without an obvious motive for the killings, police focused on a person close to Dowell as the prime suspect. But some investigators had their doubts and saw an even darker circumstance behind the slayings.

Barring an easily understandable explanation for the murders of the two teenagers, Muncie residents embraced unlikely and sometimes bizarre theories, like the one that said the slaying stemmed from a crosstown rivalry with another school. Another said that the killings grew out of Dungeons and Dragons, the popular role-playing game.

However, most chilling, to police and the public alike, was the possibility that the killer of Dixon and Dowell would never be revealed or arrested and would go unpunished, perhaps living out their life in Muncie—perhaps even as their neighbor.

As the decades wore on after the Westside Park slayings, theories continued to grow, and police continued to come back to the case. Muncie police officials periodically gave the boxes of files that stemmed from the murders to promising new investigators. One of those investigators believes he has solved the tragic crime and has focused on one man as a strong person of interest.

As the thirty-fifth anniversary of the Westside Park murders arrived, as inevitably as cold Indiana winters and hot Hoosier summers, questions remained. Chief among them was whether or not Ethan Dixon and Kimberly Dowell would find justice from the grave.

1
THE FRIDAY BEFORE

For students and faculty at Northside High School, September 27, 1985, was just another Friday. But it was a Friday that marked the end of innocence for many of them. And it was the last day of life for two of the school's students.

That morning, Ethan Dixon was wearing his standard outfit—jeans and a polo shirt—as he ambled across the parking lot of the high school's campus along Bethel Avenue on Muncie's northwest side. He spotted his friend Julie Davey slowly driving through the parking lot. Julie was a senior and Ethan was a junior, but the two had been friends since they had met while competing on the cross-country team at Storer Middle School four years earlier. Ethan tapped his hand on the hood of Julie's car.

"Hey Davey, what are you doing?" Ethan asked. "Why aren't you parking?"

Julie explained that she had come by school to drop off a neighbor who was also a student but that she was not attending classes that day. "I'm skipping school," Julie said. She told Ethan that she was driving down to southern Indiana to spend the weekend hanging out with friends. "You want to skip with me?"

Ethan smiled but declined, saying he had a test that day. Julie drove away while Ethan walked into school.

Amy Leffingwell was, like Ethan, a junior at Northside. At the end of the school day that Friday, the junior class officers met. Ethan was the class president, and Amy was the treasurer.

Left: Ethan Dixon. *Right*: Kimberly Dowell. *Author's collection.*

"After the meeting, I had a lot of questions I wanted to ask him," Amy said. "But he was busy. I waited for him, but I had to go. I thought, 'I'll just talk to him on Monday.' But then it happened."

For most Northside High School students, that Friday was like many others: get through classes without too many social faux pas and go into the weekend with as little homework as possible. The high school football season had just begun the week before, and that Friday night, Northside was playing the Jay County Patriots at the Muncie Fieldhouse Stadium. The Titans football team had lost its first game of the season.

On Friday night and Saturday night, the Northside Titans, like the Bearcats from Muncie's Central High School and the Rebels from Southside High School, could go to a game, hang out at Muncie Mall or go to a movie. *Back to the Future* was playing in its second run in Muncie at the Rivoli downtown, and Chuck Norris was starring in *Invasion USA* at the Northwest Plaza Cinema on the north side. Tickets at those and other Muncie movie theaters cost two dollars for showings before 6:00 p.m.

For the city's teenagers, the options also included going to Indian Hill, a popular hangout in the countryside near Prairie Creek Reservoir, southeast of the city. They could also sit in a car with a portable cassette player and a blanket in Westside Park—like Ethan Dixon and Kimberly Dowell did that Saturday night.

With more than three decades of hindsight, Julie Davey believes she knows what would have happened if Ethan, her fellow athlete who had often made her laugh on their four-mile runs and who also attended St. Mary's Catholic Church, had taken her up on her offer to skip school with her. "He'd still be alive," Davey said. "I grew up Catholic. I believe God has a plan. He knows when someone will pass away. I didn't feel that way. Thirty-five years later, I feel like if I could have talked him into skipping school with me, he would still be alive."

Eleven months after Ethan Dixon and Kimberly Dowell were shot to death—just a few weeks before local newspapers published stories about how the crime was still unsolved after a year and how the Muncie police acknowledged that they had made little progress toward solving the crime—a man named James "Jimmy" Swingley was pulled over by Muncie police.

Swingley had been stopped for an innocuous offense: disregarding a stop sign. The twenty-three-year-old Swingley initially gave police a false name: Kevin L. Dixon. What police didn't know at the time was that Swingley, who said his last name was that of one of the teenagers who had been killed in the park the previous fall, had told people on the night of the murders that he had pulled the trigger.

Westside Park at night and the area where the bodies of Ethan Dixon and Kimberly Dowell were found. *Courtesy of Jordan Kartholl.*

In a string of encounters on the night Ethan Dixon and Kimberly Dowell died and shortly after, Swingley told friends he had been in the park that night and what had happened. In one particularly contentious encounter, Swingley allegedly threatened an acquaintance. "I've already killed two people tonight," Swingley allegedly told the man. "I'll blow your brains out."

Jimmy Swingley would be charged with murder a few years later—but not the murders of Ethan and Kimberly.

2

THAT NIGHT

It wasn't unusual for Patrolman Terry Winters to find cars parked in the darkness at Westside Park. Winters worked the late shift for the Muncie Police Department, and on that particular night, the thirty-four-year-old K-9 officer was going to combine two duties: walk his police dog, Max, and tell people in parked cars to move along after the park closed at 11:00 p.m. The night of September 28, 1985, however, was like no other for Winters.

The patrolman was checking on vehicles sitting in the darkness at the east end of the park when he was dispatched to reports of a loud party at Colonial Crest Apartments on the western edge of the city. Winters was making his way out of the long, linear green space—along the White River west of Muncie's downtown—when he saw what looked like fresh tire tracks near the west end of the park. He followed the tracks and found a Volkswagen hatchback, parked with the engine running, and he approached the car on foot, shining his flashlight into an open window. What he saw took him so thoroughly aback that he momentarily turned off the flashlight and stood in the darkness. Then, he turned the light back on.

Inside the car were the bodies of the teenagers who were soon identified as Ethan Dixon and Kimberly Dowell. The boy had been shot in the torso, and the girl had been shot in the head. The gunshot wounds were immediately apparent. "I couldn't believe what I had just seen," Winters said in a 2014 interview with the authors, published on September 21 of that year in the *Star Press* newspaper, the successor to the *Muncie Star* and the *Muncie Evening Press*. Winters said he "immediately" called his discovery in to emergency dispatch.

In a few moments, another Muncie patrolman, Joe Winkle, arrived at the scene. Years later, Winkle became Muncie's police chief. And in a few more minutes, as the severity of the crime became clear, the scene was populated by some of the city police department's top officials, including Deputy Police Chief Marvin Campbell and investigators Lieutenant Norm Irelan and Lieutenant George Wilson. Delaware County coroner Glenn Scroggins was also there. Scroggins's brother, Donald Scroggins, was the city's police chief. The coroner himself was an experienced death investigator who had been called out to many crime scenes.

A photograph published in the *Muncie Star* on the morning of Monday, September 30, showed Campbell in a baseball jacket and cap, watching as Scroggins and Wilson looked into the car and Irelan trained a light on the interior of the vehicle. The doors of the car were open, and the shattered glass in the passenger-side window was readily apparent. The bodies of the teenagers were not visible in the photograph.

The article that accompanied the photograph—the second published, following a brief, on-deadline story in Sunday's *Star* that hadn't yet reported the names of the victims—identified Dixon and Dowell and quoted police as saying that they had been shot to death around 11:50 p.m. on Saturday. Although estimates varied, the time of their deaths was usually reported as having occurred after the park had closed at 11:00 p.m. and before midnight.

The city's homicide investigation team was at the scene throughout the night. A joint city–county homicide team, including Delaware County's sheriff's deputies, had been disbanded a few years earlier; otherwise, county officers might have helped with the investigation.

By the time the September 30 article had been published, police said that no suspects or motives were immediately apparent and that no signs of a robbery, drugs or alcohol had been found. After 9:00 p.m. that Saturday, Ethan had picked up Kimberly at her Euclid Avenue home, where she lived with her mother, Nancy, and her stepfather, Donald Vogelgesang. Kimberly's father, Muncie physician Anthony Dowell, and his wife, Sharon, lived in Indianapolis. Ethan lived with his parents, Steve and Kay Dixon, on Tyrone Drive in Muncie.

In their investigation, the police tried to determine not only who had killed Ethan and Kimberly and why but also the significance of two elements of the crime that had been discovered that night: an open knife on the dashboard of Ethan's car and a gun holster.

Campbell had been a part of the city police department since 1964. In 1985, he was Donald Scroggins's deputy chief and was in charge of the

Muncie police officers investigate Ethan Dixon's Volkswagen Rabbit at Westside Park. *Courtesy of Muncie Newspapers.*

investigations division. Campbell recalled in a 2019 interview that he lived about two blocks away from the park and that he had gotten there quickly after he was notified of the crime. "Everybody was still there, and they had the scene secured," Campbell said. "Most of the homicide team was there. They were videotaping the scene."

Campbell said that investigators interviewed Terry Winters that night, but they talked to few others, if any. "They didn't really have anybody." Winters—whose own family would experience violent tragedy a few years later—said in 2014 that the shock of his discovery that night prompted him, in part, to want to rise within the ranks of the Muncie Police Department and become a detective. That night, Winters couldn't have possibly guessed that, for decades after the killings, some in Muncie would believe he was the murderer.

Campbell, meanwhile, focused his attention and much of his investigators' energies on the man he considered to be the killer: Kimberly's stepfather.

3
WORD SPREADS

Ethan and Kimberly's deaths shocked the city of Muncie. But their friends and classmates were shaken to their souls.

"This doesn't happen here," Dan McDonald remembered thinking the night after he heard of the slayings. McDonald was a freshman at Ball State University in Muncie the night of the Westside Park killings. He had graduated from Northside High School the spring before. He knew Ethan from Northside's debate team.

Not long after McDonald heard the news, he was sitting on the porch of a house near the Ball State campus, talking to a friend. "On that front porch, I thought to myself, 'This doesn't happen here,'" McDonald recalled in a 2019 interview. "It was the sort of thing…casual violence wasn't part of our world. We were kids out playing all day long in elementary school and middle school. We didn't have cell phones. We rode our bikes and played all day long. When we were older, we were young and proud and invincible, like any teenager is."

For Amy Leffingwell, the shock of hearing about the death of her schoolmates, including her fellow class officer Ethan, came in the same way it came to many people who found out about the crime the Sunday after the killings. "I used to sleep late," Leffingwell remembered in 2019. "My parents had breakfast. My dad was at the table. The big, ginormous newspaper was on the table. The picture of the car was on the front page, and it seemed familiar. Then the phone rang, and it was my friend Jenny. I don't know if my parents were going to tell me and didn't have time."

On that newspaper's front page—across the top of the Sunday, September 29 edition of the *Muncie Star*—was a twelve-paragraph story with the headline "2 Found Dead in Parked Car." The slayings had been discovered so late on Saturday night that the newspaper didn't have the names of the two teenagers. "A young man and woman were found shot to death shortly before midnight Saturday in a car parked at Westside Park," the story began, noting that the car was a late-model Volkswagen hatchback. In the photograph, the passenger-side window is a web of broken glass with a large hole in the middle. The driver's side window, where police believed the gunman had stood and fired, was rolled down.

The article noted that Muncie police patrolman Terry Winters had found the victims and that Delaware County coroner Glenn Scroggins said that the young man had been shot in the left side of the chest. A witness told police that he saw a dark car leaving the park, while another said he saw a man with a gun running through the park. The latter tip turned out to be about a newspaper reporter carrying a portable police scanner.

Sunday morning's front-page news was seen in households throughout Muncie. In the home of Kay and Joseph Rankin, Kay read the newspaper article, not suspecting the unnamed victims in the article were two of "her" kids. Kay was the class advisor for Ethan's class and was the cheerleading sponsor for Kim and other Northside cheerleaders. Kay and Joe—the latter a longtime Muncie attorney and former city court judge—drove by Westside Park on their way to church that day. "I said, 'Oh my gosh, look at all the police activity and yellow tape,'" Kay remembered in a 2019 interview. "That must have been where it was."

After the Rankins got home from church, Kay said, "A woman I taught with called me and told me who the kids were," Kay remembered. "Oh my God. That's something you read about that happens in another community. It never happens in your community."

Today, thirty-five years later, word would spread through text messages, group chats or social media. In September 1985, however, Muncie's young people and their parents spread the word over telephone landlines, many on the kitchen wall or in teens' bedrooms. Amy Leffingwell remembered that the grim news spread quickly that Sunday, "It was just constant phone calls."

Julie Davey returned from Southern Indiana—the trip that Ethan had declined to skip school for—around 1:00 p.m. that Sunday. She said:

> *The front page of the newspaper was on the counter, and my phone was ringing. My friend Jamie said, "Have you heard the news? Kim and Ethan*

are gone." I was devastated. That night, we all came together, and we talked about it. Our memories of them. Why did this happen? Everything was so surreal. It seemed like we were all moving in slow motion. You don't expect something like that to happen in Muncie, Indiana. It's like we lost Ethan and Kim, and we lost our innocence, too.

4

THE AUTOPSIES

At 10:00 a.m. on Sunday, September 29, 1985, an autopsy was performed on Kimberly Dowell. She and Ethan Dixon were killed less than twelve hours earlier in Westside Park, and their bodies were moved from the crime scene to the pathology department at Ball Memorial Hospital, less than a mile north of the park. Ethan's autopsy was performed at 11:30 a.m. that morning. Both procedures were performed by a young pathology resident at the hospital, Gregory W. Brown, who had graduated from Indiana University School of Medicine in 1983.

The coroner in Delaware County was Glenn Scroggins, who had been elected in 1982. His one term as coroner happened to fall in the period when Dixon and Dowell were killed, but Scroggins had a long history of public service, having been a firefighter in the Muncie Fire Department. Several of his years on the department found him serving as the department's fire investigator. Scroggins's brother, Donald Scroggins, was Muncie's chief of police at the time of the Westside Park slayings, giving the family a unique position in local government at the time.

Glenn Scroggins joked, according to a December 1986 column by Joe Canan in the *Muncie Evening Press*, that "he got all his knowledge of anatomy and pathology from watching *General Hospital*," But as Canan wrote, "The fact is, he pored over medical reference books and attended every conference his paltry [office] budget could afford." In Indiana at the time—and still in 2021—it was common in many of the state's ninety-two counties that the coroners were not medical examiners or trained in medicine and pathology.

For decades, funeral home directors often served as coroners. In more recent years, Delaware County voters have elected a series of former police officers, firefighters and fire investigators as coroner. Voters prize investigative skills over medical backgrounds—and political parties obliged with nominees who had not only investigative backgrounds but also years of government service and political connections.

In Kimberly's autopsy, Brown and the cosigning Ball Memorial Hospital pathology department diplomate—a term for a doctor certified by a board of examiners—Thomas A. Kocoshis, found that "the immediate cause of death [was] a gunshot wound to the head [near] the left ear." Fragments of the bullet were found "[lodged] in the base of the skull." The autopsy's toxicology report indicated no sign of alcohol, cannabinoids, cocaine, barbiturates, opiate alkaloids, amphetamines, Quaaludes, Valium or PCP in her body. Acetaminophen traces, presumably from a headache and pain reliever, were found. The report noted that the interval "between onset and death [was] seconds."

"The deceased is a 15-year-old Caucasian female who was found in the passenger seat of a car parked with the motor running in a secluded area of Westside Park," the report noted. "Both front seats were in a reclining position with sleeping bags draped over them. The deceased was on her

Ball Memorial Hospital in the 1980s. *Courtesy of Ball State University.*

back with her arms raised above her head." Kimberly was sixty-six inches tall—about five and a half feet—and weighed 118 pounds. Emphasizing the completeness of the postmortem examination, the report noted that Kimberly's eyes were blue and that she had good oral hygiene.

In Ethan's autopsy, Brown similarly found no trace of alcohol, cannabinoids, cocaine, barbiturates, opiate alkaloids, amphetamines, PCP or other substances. "The deceased is a 16-year-old white male who was found reclining in the driver seat of his car," according to the report. "The window on his side was open. The engine was running. The deceased was lying on his back when discovered." Ethan was five feet, ten inches tall, and he weighed 135 pounds. His hair was blond, and his eyes were green. And, like Kim, his oral hygiene was good.

Ethan had been shot in the chest on his left side, near the sixth rib. His coronary artery, heart and left lung were lacerated and perforated, respectively, by the bullet. The cause of his death was a gunshot wound to the chest that caused exsanguination, or severe loss of blood. He died within minutes.

5

THE EARLY INVESTIGATION

In the wake of Ethan and Kimberly's murders, questions came more quickly than answers.

In the days following the Westside Park slayings, Muncie police fielded hundreds of calls from people who thought they saw something or knew something. "We could hardly keep track of it," Marvin Campbell, the then–deputy chief of the Muncie Police Department, recalled in a 2019 interview. At the city hall offices of the Muncie police, the phones rang, notes were taken and leads were checked. Some of them seemed promising—at first.

In the Monday, September 30 edition of the *Muncie Star*, police said they had "information" that other people were present in the park that night, and they asked them to contact the police investigations division. The article included the telephone number for the office.

Delaware County coroner Glenn Scroggins said an examination of the bullets removed during the autopsies indicated the teenagers were shot with a .38-caliber handgun. Ballistics tests were still to be completed.

The newspaper reported that Scroggins said that "a holster for a small handgun was found inside the car under Dixon's body, but a gun was not found. A pocketknife was found lying on the dashboard of the car."

On the morning of Tuesday, October 1, the *Star* reported across the top of page one, "Slayings might involve 3, police say." Muncie police lieutenant David Nicholson said that investigators had been told as many as three people had been seen around the car after shots were fired. Police also said that a vehicle, reportedly seen near Ethan's car, had left the park quickly after shots were fired. As many as a dozen cars were in the park at the time of the shootings, estimated around 11:00 p.m. By the time the article was published, the owners of eight of those cars had been identified.

Scroggins said three shots were fired: two of the shots hit the victims, and the third shattered the passenger-side window near Kimberly.

The article ended with another plea from police that anyone with information about the case call investigators.

By Thursday, October 3, the *Muncie Star* was reporting that the death investigation was focusing on two cars and their drivers. Campbell was quoted as saying, "One of them has got to be a damn good witness, and the other one is a suspect." One car was a dark vehicle that was sometimes referred to as a Chevrolet Monte Carlo in accounts of that night.

Three people who were interviewed as potential witnesses said that they had heard gunshots but didn't call police. "Some of them got scared and decided to get the hell out," Campbell told the newspaper.

Police Chief Donald Scroggins, addressing rumors that were sweeping Muncie, said police believed they could rule out a random killer. Police also discounted the rumors of a feud that stemmed from an earlier fight involving Ethan or that the slayings were connected to the popular role-playing game Dungeons and Dragons.

Marvin Campbell, deputy chief of the Muncie Police Department in 1985. *Author's collection.*

Later in the week, Muncie mayor James P. Carey pledged $5,000 to start a reward fund to solve the crime. Carey, a former Muncie police chief and Delaware County sheriff, also urged anyone with information about the slayings to contact him personally.

Tips called in to the police about the killings came in so fast that investigators could hardly keep up. One person the police briefly considered but later eliminated as a suspect was the owner of a prominent Muncie restaurant. The man was considered, Campbell said in a 2019 interview, because he was well known for shooting at a local gun range.

Campbell also said that a deputy marshal from a smaller nearby town came forward to say that he was in Westside Park that night and thought he could identify a suspect. "He was in the park when it went down," Campbell said. "It was Monday or Tuesday when he came in and volunteered that. He basically described the guy in the car, which we believed to be Vogelgesang," referring to Kimberly Dowell's stepfather, Donald Vogelgesang. Campbell said Vogelgesang had gone to Westside Park that night in the hours after the teenagers were shot to death. The stepfather, when he was stopped at the entrance to the park by a city police officer, asked what had happened. The officer told him that two people had been shot but that the identities of the victims had not yet been released.

According to Campbell, in his interview with Muncie police a few days after the slayings, the deputy marshal said he had been parked in Westside Park with a woman who was not his wife before the shootings. "He was down there with some girl, making out," Campbell said about the deputy marshal. "A car pulled up beside him…he looked at [the deputy] like, 'Who the fuck are you?' [The deputy] thought, 'Fuck you,' and stared back at him. He drove off." Campbell said the deputy marshal was interviewed under hypnosis and said he believed the car that pulled up near his vehicle continued on to the area where, minutes later, Ethan and Kimberly were shot.

A couple who was also in the park that night identified photographs of a car that police believed to be Vogelgesang's, Campbell said, but they couldn't identify the driver.

Campbell quickly came to focus on Vogelgesang as the prime suspect in the case and asked the stepfather to come to city hall to be interviewed. Muncie police lieutenant George Wilson questioned Vogelgesang in a polygraph, or lie detector, exam. "He said he didn't see any deception," Campbell recalled. "I said, 'Bullshit, George."

Campbell said, "When I followed up on the polygraph, I asked [the stepfather], 'Were you in the park?' He said, 'Within my body, I wasn't there.' I asked him, 'What the fuck are you talking about? You were either there or not there.' He said it again. 'Within my body, I wasn't there.'" In interviews in the years following the killings, police sources said that Vogelgesang also said something to the effect of, "If I was there, you'll have to tell me I was there."

Michael J. "Mick" Alexander was Delaware County's prosecuting attorney at the time of the slayings. Campbell consulted with Alexander's longtime friend and deputy prosecutor Richard Reed, who suggested Campbell should ask a local psychologist what Vogelgesang might have meant. Campbell did. "He didn't know."

Campbell and Jack Stonebraker, a veteran police investigator who was later elected Delaware County coroner, took the text of their interviews to the Southern Police Institute in Louisville, where an investigator told them the statements were of a "control freak" who was unlikely to talk to police again.

When police tried to schedule a follow-up interview with Vogelgesang on the Saturday after the killings, they were advised by the stepfather's attorney, Charles "Chic" Clark, that his client would not be sitting down with police again.

"When I was interviewing Vogelgesang...there are about 10 [indicators] when somebody is lying," Campbell said in 2019. "They're jittery, they're sweating, their mouth is dry. He met six of them. I interviewed a lot of bad people. Murderers, rapists, you name it. Boy, he sure fit the profile for somebody who was lying, but who knows?" Campbell added with a tone of sarcasm in his voice.

Campbell said that if the couple had been able to identify more than just the car they saw in the park that night, if they had been able to positively identify Vogelgesang, "I would have arrested him."

"They all said he's a nice guy, he wouldn't do it," Campbell said. "Bullshit. Nice people kill."

While Muncie investigators followed up on tips and conducted interviews—and while Campbell focused on Kimberly's stepfather—police released a sketch of a man who witnesses said they saw in the park that night. In the decades that followed, police never publicly associated a name with the sketch. In the 2019 interview, Campbell identified the man in the sketch as James "Jimmy" Swingley.

6
BACK TO SCHOOL

The Monday after the Saturday night that Ethan Dixon and Kimberly Dowell were killed in Westside Park, Northside High School classes were back in session. It was anything but a typical school day.

Amy Leffingwell remembered the shock of the realization that her friend Ethan was dead. "His desk was empty," Leffingwell recalled in a 2019 interview. "I had a lot of classes with Ethan…his desk was empty." Leffingwell doesn't remember any kind of large-scale meeting of students, faculty and counselors. "I don't think they gathered us in a group. If you wanted to talk to somebody, you could, but mostly, we talked among ourselves."

"It was probably the worst day of my teaching career," Kay Rankin, Kim's cheerleading sponsor, remembered in 2019. "Worse than the shuttle exploding and 9-11 and Oklahoma City. Because this was home."

Ethan's friend Julie Davey was, on the Monday after the killings, working in the school office during her free period. Her job was to collect and record student body attendance. "The secretary in the office asked if I could disenroll them from school, Kim and Ethan," Davey recalled. "She said, 'I just can't do it.' I had to take their information and pull their paperwork and put it in another file. I remember an odd, cold feeling. Ethan was my friend."

Davey and Leffingwell remembered that students gathered outside school hours to talk about the loss of their friends. "We all came together and talked about it," Davey said. "Our memories of them. Why did this happen?"

Northside High School. *Courtesy of Keith Roysdon.*

The Tuesday after the killings, separate funerals were held for Kim and Ethan. Kim's was held on Tuesday afternoon in High Street United Methodist Church in downtown Muncie, while Ethan's had been held that morning in St. Mary's Catholic Church on the city's west side. Calling hours for the two were held early that Monday evening at Meeks Mortuary downtown.

Leffingwell went to the calling hours and, because she knew him better, the funeral services for Ethan. "I couldn't believe looking into a casket and seeing someone I had known since middle school, and someone so smart and funny was just…gone. I remember looking at Kim, and I thought she looked odd," Leffingwell said. "I remember bright blue eye shadow. We all wore bright blue eye shadow, but it was just too much."

Davey remembered the long funeral processions for Ethan and Kimberly, and she recalled that she was interviewed by an Indianapolis TV reporter. "You don't expect something like that to happen in Muncie, Indiana." Davey said. "Nowadays, people are numb about things. We hear every detail of everything that happens around the world. But this…it's like we not only lost Ethan and Kim, we lost our innocence, too."

"I went to Kim's funeral," Rankin remembered. "Some of the cheerleaders were with me. Our athletic director asked if I was going to the mortuary. He said, 'Don't go by yourself.' It turns out, he was the one who couldn't go by himself."

With the funerals over, Northside students and faculty returned to school and tried to settle into a routine.

"Then the rumors started flying," Leffingwell said.

A VIOLENT HISTORY

Long before he was a convicted murderer, James Lee Swingley lived a life marked by violent death and crime. In his early years, the violence was not of his own doing.

On Friday, June 9, 1972, a little after noon, Swingley's eight-year-old sister, Cindy Ann, dashed out of the yard in front of the family's Powers Street home and into oncoming traffic. She was struck by an automobile driven by a southside Muncie man, newspapers reported. The second grader at Jefferson Elementary School suffered multiple injuries. A journalism graduate student at Ball State University who saw the accident in his rearview mirror stopped and tried to give the unconscious girl artificial respiration, but she died just after 4:00 p.m. at Ball Memorial Hospital. Among her survivors were her brothers, who were identified in a newspaper account as Jackie D. and James L. "Jimmy" Swingley. The latter, born in September 1962, was nine years old when his sister was killed.

Nearly a decade later, on Tuesday, January 27, 1981, Jack (Jackie) D. Swingley was arguing with his wife, Becky, in their home at 723 South Jefferson Street when she struck him in the head with a cigarette lighter, according to newspaper accounts. Jack Swingley staggered, collapsed and quickly died, and Delaware County coroner Larry Cole, a physician, initially ruled the death a homicide. But investigators later determined that Swingley had died from a brain hemorrhage that was not caused by the blow. The lighter struck him in the temple, but the hemorrhage occurred at the base of his skull. Officials revised the cause of death to "undetermined."

Newspaper accounts noted that Jack Swingley and his brother, Jimmy, had been "drinking heavily all day." Jack Swingley was twenty and Jimmy Swingley was eighteen years old at the time. The nature of the dispute that day is known only to the Swingley brothers and Jack's wife, Becky. But Desiree Dawn, the mother of Jack and Jimmy Swingley, would many years later confirm to Muncie police investigator Nathan Sloan that a little more than nine months after Jack's death, Becky gave birth to a child fathered by Jimmy Swingley.

8

MORE INVESTIGATION, MORE MURDERS

On Sunday, October 6, 1985—the day after Kimberly Dowell's stepfather, Don Vogelgesang, was supposed to talk to police investigators but did not on the advice of his attorney—the *Muncie Star* updated readers on the Westside Park investigation at the one-week mark.

Muncie police lieutenant David Nicholson told the newspaper that investigators were working fourteen to sixteen hours a day and "interviewing people all the time," but no progress had been made. "We have nothing new today," Nicholson said.

A dozen "new sources" had been interviewed, Nicholson was quoted as saying. "We're picking up people, bringing them in and interviewing them. After we talk to them, they've been released." One of the three possible suspects had been interviewed, Muncie deputy police chief Marvin Campbell told the newspaper. That person had been advised of their rights.

Nicholson said the case was hard to solve because there were virtually no clues. The newspaper article cited the knife that had been found on the dashboard of Ethan's Volkswagen Rabbit and the gun holster that had been found under the young man. The investigator also said that police had received some strange calls, including one that blamed the deaths on Klingons, the warlike alien race from *Star Trek*. Nicholson said he told the caller that the Klingons hadn't been heard from since *Star Trek* was canceled.

The reward for information leading to an arrest had grown to $10,000, with $5,000 being offered by Mayor James P. Carey and another $5,000 being offered by American National Bank officials. The public was invited to contribute to the reward fund through Merchants National Bank offices.

Campbell revealed to the newspaper that a polygraph test had been given to the driver of a car in the park that night. (In 2019, Campbell said that the driver was Don Vogelgesang, Kimberly Dowell's stepfather.) In the meantime, two men in a black car were being sought. Twelve to fifteen officers were working on the case at the time, Campbell said.

In a 2019 interview, Campbell said the police even consulted with a psychic in Indianapolis who led them to briefly suspect the owner of a popular Muncie restaurant. "We couldn't tie him to it," Campbell said. Police also checked on theories that said Ethan Dixon's killing had somehow been drug related. "We couldn't find any kids saying they were involved in drugs," Campbell said. The possibility of a drug-related motive to the crime was explored again many years later.

Within a few weeks of the slayings of Ethan and Kimberly, Muncie police found themselves investigating another double homicide. In this instance, however, a resolution was quick in coming.

On Thursday, December 5, 1985, two women, thirty-seven-year-old Carol Revis and her sixteen-year-old daughter, Wendi Matson, were shot and killed in their South Eaton Avenue home. Police quickly arrested and prosecutors charged their twenty-year-old neighbor, James Randall Campbell, for the murders. Matson was identified as Campbell's "sometime girlfriend." Campbell had threatened Matson, and police said he kicked in the door of their home and first shot the mother, then the daughter.

In May 1986, Delaware Superior Court 1 judge Robert Barnet Jr. sentenced Campbell to 120 years in prison. At the time, this was a record sentence out of Delaware County. Campbell had earlier confessed to the crime.

Near the end of December 1985, Marvin Campbell and other officials reflected, for an article in the *Muncie Star*, on the violent year that had taken its toll on Muncie's young people. The deaths of Matson and her mother were cited, but chief among the year's violent events was the Westside Park case.

FEAR AND LOATHING IN MUNCIE—AND FLORIDA

O n Monday, October 7, 1985, Deputy Police Chief Marvin Campbell released a composite sketch of a man who was wanted for questioning in connection with the shooting of Dixon and Dowell. The drawing showed a man with glasses and hair parted in the middle. According to the *Muncie Evening Press*:

> *He is described as a white male, about five feet ten inches tall, weighing 150 to 160 pounds. He is about 24 years old, has dark brown hair parted in the middle and feathered back on the sides, has a slender build and a thin face with severe acne marks. He has no facial hair and wore gold wire-framed eyeglasses. The car is a black Monte Carlo (Chevrolet, model year approximately 1972–75) jacked up with wide tires on the rear and Cragar magnesium wheels. The car had dual exhaust and there may be a feather with a roach clip (marijuana smoking device) attached hanging on the rear-view mirror.*

In a 2019 interview, Campbell said the sketch was later determined by police to be of James "Jimmy" Swingley. The newspaper reported that the man "may be either a witness to or a suspect in the double killing." Campbell said at least two people were in the black car, which left the park "quickly after the shots were heard."

The deputy chief said police were also checking on rumors that Ethan "may have had a confrontation with a teenager on the south side of town."

Campbell also said that police had confirmed that Ethan and Kimberly were "invited" to a Ball State University fraternity party on Saturday night, but there was no indication that they had attended. Campbell said a person "close" to the victims had been questioned and given a lie detector test, which was inconclusive.

A person of interest sketch released by the Muncie Police Department in October 1985. *Author's collection.*

The following day, on October 8, the *Muncie Evening Press* published a drawing, laying out the location of Ethan's Volkswagen hatchback in the park. Police said the sketch published the day before had prompted one hundred phone calls and tips from the public.

Police said they had interviewed most of the dozen people they initially wanted to speak to and had crossed them off their lists of potential suspects.

Later in the week, police said lab tests determined that gunshot residue was found on both Ethan and Kimberly, leading investigators to believe their killer was standing very close to the teenagers when he shot them—and that perhaps he even held the gun inside the car as he pulled the trigger.

For weeks after the deaths of Ethan and Kimberly, rumors, consternation and, in some cases, outright fear swept through Muncie's young population. "We were consumed that they didn't know who did it," Amy Leffingwell recalled. "We desperately wanted someone to be caught because we were scared," she added. "We thought maybe someone had it out for kids at Northside because there was no logical explanation. Still isn't. We thought we would be next, we didn't feel safe. Sometimes, when I was in my room, I thought, 'Who is going to be next?'" A friend and classmate gave Leffingwell the scare of her life by standing outside her bedroom window and "banging" on it. "I rolled off my bed and army crawled into the living room to get my father."

"I was not fearful at all," Julie Davey recalled. But Davey does remember the rumors that circulated around the city. "I remember for a long time, they said a black Monte Carlo [was a car seen in the park that night]," Davey said. "Do you know how many black Monte Carlos there were in Muncie? A lot." Police said in early October 1985 that five hundred Monte Carlos were owned in Delaware County. "Then the police officer…then you heard her [stepdad] did it…all these conspiracy theories."

Leffingwell said kids in her circles thought that a drug dealer killed Ethan and Kim.

Kay Rankin, Northside's cheerleading sponsor, said rumors were rampant. "There were all these rumors flying that Kim's stepdad was responsible," Rankin said.

> *Two weeks afterward, I had to go to their house to pick up Kim's*
> *cheerleading uniform. You know how you can sense tension or that*
> *something's not right? I never felt any of that. None of that. I don't think*
> *he had anything to do with it. I think they saw something they shouldn't*
> *have seen, or somebody thought they saw something. I think the police*
> *know who did it, and they can't prove it. I think they know who did it but*
> *just don't have the evidence. That's just my gut.*

Even in shocked and sorrowful Muncie, life went on. Ball State University's homecoming festivities were held in the week following the slayings. A Hollywood production company, Hemdale, was looking for extras to go to the Knightstown Junior-Senior High School gymnasium south of Muncie for a casting session for the Gene Hackman basketball movie *Hoosiers*. In the first dozen days of October, film legends Orson Welles and Yul Brynner died, meriting front-page stories in the *Muncie Star*.

Sometime in the days or weeks following the Westside Park slayings, Jimmy Swingley left his friends, acquaintances and family in Muncie and went to Florida. Swingley told an informant for a police agency other than the Muncie Police Department that he had been with two men on September 28, 1985, one of whom had killed Dixon and Dowell in Westside Park. Swingley told the informant that he was leaving Muncie for Florida.

Swingley was, from accounts related to Muncie police around 2014, living under a highway overpass while he was in Florida. He apparently didn't know anyone in the state who he would have been visiting. However, his lack of acquaintances in Florida didn't stop him from getting into trouble. Swingley was arrested in Florida on December 5, 1985, after he held a knife to the throat of a man. The man had taunted Swingley, saying that he would not follow through on a boast of going to Australia.

MUNCIE IN 1985

What was the city of Muncie like in September 1985, when the lives of Kimberly Dowell and Ethan Dixon were taken in Westside Park? It's likely that some people who hadn't been in the city since thirty-five years before, in 1950, wouldn't have recognized Muncie. Likewise, Muncie today, thirty-five years after the Westside Park slayings, is a very different community.

Muncie's population has taken some dramatic turns over this seventy-year period. Fueled by industrial growth and plentiful jobs, the city's population had grown to 58,479 in 1950, an increase of nearly 10,000 people in the ten years between 1940 and 1950. By 1980, the population was 77,216, perhaps its peak. By 2019, the population had dropped to 68,529.

Emigration helped fuel this decrease in population, and some of that was sparked by the loss of jobs that had once been sought after, including industrial jobs, like those at Warner Gear (later BorgWarner Automotive), Chevrolet Muncie, Delco, Ball Brothers, Westinghouse and other large plants. Warner Gear was the king of industrial employers in Muncie, with more than five thousand workers in the 1950s.

The area, settled by the Lenape people in the 1790s, became the state of Indiana's newest city in 1865. Natural gas fueled industrial development in the late 1800s, but the natural gas reserves were exhausted within a few years, and the "gas boom" was over by 1910. The city's greatest natural resource soon became its people. Muncie residents, many of who were part of the southern migration to northern states in the first half of the twentieth century, worked in auto parts factories and other types of manufacturing facilities, as well as in service jobs and in healthcare and higher education. Once BorgWarner, the last of the sizable manufacturers, closed in 2009, the city's largest employers were Ball State University, Ball Memorial Hospital and local government offices and schools.

Muncie became known as "Little Chicago"—a name "claimed" by other midwestern cities—in the twentieth century, due to perceptions of political corruption and sometimes lawlessness in the city. The authors' books *Wicked Muncie* and *Muncie Murder & Mayhem*, published by Arcadia and The History Press, recount dozens of true crime stories from Muncie's history.

As 1985 began, city and Delaware County officials struggled to agree on plans for a public safety complex that would include a new jail and police offices. The project was initiated in the wake of a federal court lawsuit, filed in 1978 by jail inmates, over conditions in the old jail. Within four years, Mayor James P. Carey's withdrawal of city participation in the project led to the construction and opening of the Justice Center, a courts-and-jail complex, in 1992. In 2019, county officials were moving forward with the building of a new jail to replace the Justice Center.

Walnut Street in downtown Muncie during a failed attempt to turn the street into a pedestrian mall (after 1975). *Courtesy of Ball State University.*

In 1985, two firefighters filed a $20 million lawsuit, alleging that Carey and other officials used political favoritism to make promotions in the Muncie Fire Department. The chamber of commerce hoped an Ohio businessman would follow through on his promises to create three hundred jobs by opening a sugar processing plant in the former Marhoefer Packing Company building, which had been empty since the company declared bankruptcy in 1978. (The plan didn't come to fruition.)

Observers of the local business scene were correct in theorizing that the community's commercial development would move toward the west, along McGalliard Road and Indiana 332. The Lyndenbrook Place commercial and business development was growing, and as one business owner said in 1985, "There's a lot of growth, and it's coming in our direction."

Downtown, hope sprang eternal—but without much reason to do so. Muncie Mall had opened on the city's northeast side in 1970 and was still thriving, but downtown boosters were still trying to get new development and renovation going, with improvements to the Wysor, Patterson and Odd Fellows buildings planned. Within a few years, the Wysor was razed, and the redevelopment of the others took additional decades. One scheme to revitalize downtown—which didn't work—was a 1975 decision to close Walnut Street, a major north–south artery in the heart of the city, and build a pedestrian mall. It was a practice that had caught on in other cities, but it was decades before new businesses and redevelopment came to downtown Muncie.

Muncie Community Schools struggled with its finances and considered closing a school—a forecast that would come true when Northside High School closed in 1988. Enrollment in local schools was in freefall, and by 2019, Muncie Community Schools had closed several other buildings and had one remaining high school, Central. Northside became a middle school.

Local tourism officials said they hoped to mount a billboard campaign based on Muncie's celebrities, including Jim Davis, the creator of *Garfield*, and broadcaster David Letterman, a Ball State graduate. Decades later, the city still featured the two in promotional materials.

As time churned on and the Westside Park slayings became a dim memory for some, Muncie became hardly recognizable to a visitor from 1950—or even 1985.

A SCHOOL IN CONTROVERSY

Muncie's Northside High School was mired in controversy before it opened, as well as when it closed.

The school was seen by some as a haven for the children of the city's elite—doctors and lawyers, business owners and Ball State University professors—and it never overcame that image, even among students.

Muncie's Central High School, initially just Muncie High School, had operated for nearly a century—since 1868—before the second Muncie Community Schools upper-grades facility, Southside High School, was opened in September 1962. (Burris Laboratory School had opened in 1929 as a place, in part, for education majors at Ball State University to get their training. It was not and is not a part of Muncie Community Schools.) Not long after Southside was opened, Muncie Community Schools officials and a few community leaders began talking about a new, northside high school.

Because of the nature of the city—divided by railroad tracks and cultural lines into blue-collar homes on the south side, African American homes on the northeast side and upper-middle-class homes radiating from the Ball State University campus on the northwest side—it was soon obvious that the new northside school would, for the most part, cater to upper-middle-class families from its location along Bethel Avenue.

"Either your parent was a teacher, a doctor, a professor at Ball State, a judge," Julie Davey said. "Everybody at Northside, their parent was somebody."

"We were the goody-two-shoes," Amy Leffingwell said. "People thought we were privileged, entitled, stuck up, even though we all weren't. Anyone that said they went to Northside got eye rolls. 'Oh, is your dad a doctor?' I finally got to saying, 'I go to Northside, but I'm not rich.'"

Kay Rankin, who taught at Central beginning in 1968 and then at Northside from 1971 until the school closed in 1988, said that it was perhaps never publicly announced that Northside would be a school for the children of parents who didn't want them to attend Muncie schools with "lower-class" children, "but that was always the idea behind it." She said, "The very influential people in Muncie were behind the building of the school."

Rankin acknowledged that Central High School, before Northside was opened, was overcrowded. "They needed a new school. We were busting at the seams. We had 2,500 in that building. But did they need a new school or just a new Muncie Central? If they just built the new Central, we wouldn't have had that division. The school board divided the city into north, east, south and west by the names of the schools."

The local school system took the first step toward Northside High School in 1965, when it purchased about seventeen acres of land at Bethel and Oakwood Avenues. Planning for the new school formally began in March 1966.

Construction began in January 1969, under Baystone Construction, the same construction company that, two decades later, was chosen to build the Delaware County Justice Center, a courts-and-jail complex that was infamous for its design and construction problems. But Northside, which, at 189,000 square feet, included an auditorium, swimming pool and classrooms for 670, had no extraordinary construction problems. Instead, the building's birth was marked by a lawsuit, which was filed by African American families in U.S. District Court in Indianapolis. The judge in the case refused to halt construction, however, and his decision was upheld in appeals court.

The new school was dedicated in December 1970.

But enrollment in Muncie schools, driven downward by population loss and the loss of local industrial jobs, fell through the decades. In 1987, the school's superintendent proposed that Northside be made into a middle school and that its student population be sent, for the most part, to a more recent vintage Central High School building, which had been opened in 1974.

Northside's closing meant there was a better racial balance among the local schools, the superintendent argued, and the larger remaining schools provided more opportunities for students. The announcement prompted refrains of "we told you so" among people who noted that, even in the 1960s, concerns about declining enrollment indicated that the city didn't need Central, Southside and Northside High Schools.

"Some of us are scared about going to Central," one Northside student was quoted as saying in a May 1988 article in the *Muncie Evening Press*. "It'll be a new situation. It's just something that's going to have to happen."

Northside High School closed on June 7, 1988. It reopened in the fall as Northside Middle School.

"The kids referred to Northside as the preppy school," Rankin said. "Everybody wore Izod. I had the cheerleaders, and the majority of my cheerleaders came from affluent homes. I had the doctors' daughters, the car dealers' daughters. They always had the Gucci purses. But you know what? They were just teenagers."

"ETHAN GOT WHAT HE DESERVED"

K imberly Dowell's mother, Nancy Vogelgesang, received one of the cruelest telephone calls imaginable not long after her daughter and Ethan Dixon were shot to death in Westside Park. A young man's voice on the other end of the phone spoke to chilling effect that Kimberly had been an innocent bystander that night in the park. "I'm sorry she was shot, but Ethan got exactly what he deserved," the man said.

The call was recounted by a person close to Nancy Vogelgesang to a Muncie police investigator nearly twenty-eight years after the two teenagers were killed. It was one of a number of upsetting calls—and it likely was intended to hurt rather than comfort—that family members or people who were close to the Dixon and Dowell families received in the days, weeks and months after Ethan and Kimberly were killed. It was, however, the only call of its type known to latter-day investigators.

Nearly three decades after the fact, police knew it would be virtually impossible to determine the nature of the call or, for that matter, the identity of the caller.

At whatever point Nancy Vogelgesang answered that phone call, she had undoubtedly been through the worst trials that a mother could suffer. Not only had her daughter been killed, but her husband, Don, Kim's stepfather, was the subject of a police investigation that tried, without success, to pin the killings on him. Marvin Campbell, the deputy police chief, had focused on Don Vogelgesang early in the investigation and made references—without publicly citing the stepfather's name—to a person "close to the victims" in interviews with newspaper reporters.

Nancy Vogelgesang, for her part, defended her husband. She said he had arrived home from a Yorktown football game before the shootings and didn't go out again that night until about 12:30 a.m., after Nancy expressed concern for Kim, who hadn't returned home by her 11:00 p.m. curfew. The teenagers were killed after 11:00 p.m., when Don Vogelgesang would have been home by his own wife's account.

In interviews years later, which were conducted through Don's attorney, Charles "Chic" Clark, Don Vogelgesang not only maintained his innocence but also complained that the police focus on him—even though his name was off the record when police gave interviews to newspaper reporters—had stymied the investigation. "If they had properly conducted a vigorous investigation of the facts

Donald Vogelgesang, the stepfather of Kimberly Dowell. *Author's collection.*

that they had and had listened to what Nancy and I had to say, I am convinced the killer or killers would now be in jail," Vogelgesang said in a 1997 interview. "It was easier to follow one man's preconceived notion that it had to be the stepfather, rather than get down to the hard work of solving a horrible crime."

Nancy Vogelgesang gave her own statement to attorney Clark. "To me, this is a nightmare that not in one's wildest dreams could be made up. I want to know what happened that night, and I would not protect anybody to solve this murder."

Kay Rankin, a Northside teacher and Kim's cheerleading sponsor, said she didn't believe the rumors about Don Vogelgesang. But she agreed that the toll on Nancy Vogelgesang and the other parents was a great one. "It's one of those things you can't get over," Rankin said. "It's a parent's worst nightmare. I think a lot of things went to the grave [with Nancy]. So many people were so suspicious of Don Vogelgesang. She's the one who would know. I think she would have felt that."

Nancy Vogelgesang died on Christmas Eve in 1987, a little more than two years after her daughter was killed in Westside Park. She was attending candlelight services at High Street United Methodist Church when she had a heart attack. She died shortly after her arrival at Ball Memorial Hospital. Her funeral service was held at the church where her daughter's funeral service had been held more than two years earlier.

MOVIE THEATERS, CRUISING AND HANGING OUT

I n 1985, if you were a teenager living in a city that was the same size and in the same geographic location as Muncie, you probably complained that there was nothing to do. And then you found something to do anyway. Sometimes, this "something" was sitting in a parked car in a quiet spot. Other times, it was something decidedly noisier and less solitary.

When Ethan Dixon and Kimberly Dowell decided to sit in Ethan's car in Westside Park on the fateful night of September 28, they weren't sitting in an indoor movie theater. Muncie had several at the time, including Movies at Muncie Mall, Northwest Plaza Cinema, Delaware Cinema and the Rivoli, the city's last downtown movie theater. Two dollars would get young moviegoers into most of the city's movie theaters, particularly before 6:00 p.m. The movies playing that weekend ran the gamut from comedy to action. Martial arts star Chuck Norris lays waste to bad guys in *Invasion USA*, which was playing at Northwest Plaza, while young star Kevin Costner rides into town in *Silverado* at Movies at Muncie Mall.

Muncie's two outdoor theaters, the Ski-Hi Drive-In north of the city and the Muncie Drive-in on the city's west side, had offered open-air movies—and a chance to cuddle, make out or more—since the 1940s and 1950s. Tom Hanks was starring in the comedy *The Man with One Red Shoe* at the Ski-Hi, while Goldie Hawn was starring in *Protocol* at the Muncie Drive-In in September 1985. A few miles north of Muncie, outside Hartford City, the Blackford County Drive-In offered X-rated "adult" movies to patrons who were twenty-one years of age and older.

The Blackford County Drive-In, north of Muncie, which showed "adult" movies. *Author's collection.*

Exactly two weeks before the Westside Park slayings, the *Muncie Star* newspaper ran an article titled "Weekends in Muncie Can Be Fun—No Foolin,'" which detailed for Ball State University students coming to the community for the first time the activities available for "the young people." Muncie had one "under twenty-one" club called No Bar and Grill; it was located in the village commercial area along University Avenue near the college campus. For $2.00, young people could hear local bands play rock and pop music at the club. Sultan's Castle was the city's best-known and longest-living video and pinball arcade. Tucked away in a wing of Muncie Mall, Sultan's Castle offered, for a quarter per play, the latest games. The Putting Cup, not far from the mall, was the city's remaining miniature golf course, where young people and families knocked balls around eighteen holes for $1.25.

Dixon and Dowell, who never reached the age of twenty-one, likely didn't spend much time at Muncie's bars that were targeted at young adults. King's Corner, near the Northwest Plaza Cinema, was perhaps the king of local dance venues. But almost every bar had its own customer base, particularly the Chug, Mugly's and Dash Riprock's in the village near Ball State.

"Wholesome" activities for young people included two roller-skating rinks, Gibson's on the city's south side and Skateaway on McGalliard Road, farther east of Muncie Mall.

For a little more than a dollar a gallon—the national average at the time, although prices certainly fluctuated—teens could gas up their cars and cruise Madison Street. Like a lot of cities, Muncie had popular stretches of roadway where teens and young adults liked to cruise. In Muncie, the most popular was a section of Madison Street that stretched from near downtown to the Southway Plaza Shopping Center at the city's southern boundary. Over this stretch of some twenty blocks, teens tooled slowly up and down, back and forth, for hours at a time, stopping to get refills of gas and pop. All this cruising didn't amount to much for the fast-food restaurants and convenience stores, like Village Pantry, along Madison Street. The teens weren't spending much money, as they were counting their nickels and dimes to put a couple of gallons in their tanks.

Madison Street cruising had long been a source of irritation for some. In April 1980, the *Muncie Evening Press* reported on city police's "concerted war" on Madison Street cruising. Looking for illegal drugs or weapons, police used violations of city noise ordinances, failures to turn on headlights or moving violations, like speeding, to pull over and search cars. "Loitering juveniles" were hustled out of the parking lots of Madison Street businesses.

Not every Muncie cop felt strongly about Madison Street cruising. Captain William Kirkman of the Juvenile Affairs Division said he wasn't certain it was a good idea to not allow teens to gather. "They are always going to have someplace to congregate," Kirkman told the *Evening Press*. And some of those places, Kirkman indicated, were unsavory when compared to Madison Street.

INDIAN HILL

Far from Westside Park, along busy White River Boulevard, the young people of Muncie and Delaware County enjoyed a remote gathering place that was, for decades, a concern and a place of consternation for local police.

Outside Muncie's city limits was the biggest park "in" the city. The City of Muncie owned the park land surrounding Prairie Creek Reservoir, a man-made lake that was created in the late 1950s. The reservoir provided water for the area and was owned by a water utility company. The park land around the reservoir, including Indian Hill, a few miles southeast of the city, was city property and its maintenance and public safety were the responsibility of the city.

In 1980, as police talked about teenagers cruising Madison Street, they noted that Indian Hill was a popular place for young people to gather. Captain William Kirkman of the Muncie Police Department's Juvenile Aid Division noted that Indian Hill had been the scene of arrests, including some for liquor law violations, just a few days before the interview. It was common for hundreds of young people to gather, drink and play music at Indian Hill on the west side of the reservoir along County Road 475-East. "It's fine to go out there and have fun, but they'll have to leave the drinks at home," Kirkman told the *Muncie Evening Press*.

Indian Hill had always been a place to gather—and sometimes, it was a problem. Over the Fourth of July weekend in 1965, Civil War reenactors gathered at Indian Hill and fired off small cannons and muzzle-loading rifles.

Prairie Creek Reservoir, a city park southeast of Muncie. *Courtesy of Ball State University.*

But in July 1972, "off limits" signs were posted around Indian Hill and other stretches of the reservoir. Muncie police were trying to control nighttime crowds and partiers at the popular spot. Fishermen could still access the area, police said, but from 10:00 p.m. to 6:00 a.m., cars and, particularly, the cars of young revelers were not allowed around Indian Hill and other nearby areas. Signs had been posted before but were stolen by Indian Hill partiers, authorities said, adding that there had been "a lot of trouble" with large drinking parties.

The very remoteness of Indian Hill made it attractive to lawbreakers, miscreants and those who, either by design or accident, found themselves on the wrong side of the authorities' favor. In May 1979, two men were arrested for fighting at Indian Hill. In August 1989, a Muncie woman reported she was raped at Indian Hill. In September 1999, park security officers found a car abandoned near Indian Hill. Not far away, the body of a fifty-seven-year-old woman was found. Police said she committed suicide.

Sometimes, Indian Hill's solitude was prized for all the right reasons. In April 1986, a local astronomy teacher led a group of students to the spot, far from city lights, to watch a comet. "Airhead," shouted one of the crowd's members at a passing car, whose headlights infringed on the night sky.

THE MALL WAS KING

I n 1985, Muncie teenagers had choices ranging from home videos and record albums to concerts and movies to entertain themselves. But for its role as a gathering place—a place to shop, eat and see movies—Muncie Mall was king.

Opened on Muncie's northeast side in 1970, Muncie Mall, like most indoor shopping malls, was a draw for teens and young people. The nation's first enclosed mall, the Southdale Center in Edina, Minnesota, opened in 1956. By the 1980s, malls were ubiquitous, with some of the largest malls being located in the Midwest, like Castleton Square in Indianapolis and Glenbrook Square in Fort Wayne, drawing shoppers from all over the state.

Muncie Mall had something those two malls didn't as far as the city's teens were concerned: proximity. Parents could drop young teenagers off at the mall and trust they were safe for a few hours. Car-driving teens, with their own mobility and independence, could make their own way to the mall—assuming they weren't using the mall as cover for sneaking out to some other spot.

Muncie's Mall, for decades, was owned by the Simon family—purveyors of some of the largest and most popular malls in the Midwest. When it opened, the mall had a general purpose: to be a for-the-entire-family shopping center, with grocery stores and drugstores. But by the 1980s, the mall had focused more squarely on young consumers and teenagers who, even if they didn't have money, could walk around the mall, talking with friends and flirting with other young people.

Muncie Mall in the 1980s. *Courtesy of Ball State University.*

The mall's popularity took a toll on downtown Muncie, which saw anchor stores like Sears and J.C. Penney move to the mall and forsake downtown. No one could blame the merchants, really; malls were the place to be.

Muncie Mall, in 1985, had a lineup of stores that were intended to draw young people not only on the weekend but also, for those with parents who would allow, early evenings throughout the rest of the week. High among the mall's draws was the United Artists Movie Theater at the back of the shopping center. Accessible from the mall—until the retail stores closed for the night—or the mall's back parking lot, the three-screen theater showed not only the movie industry's latest hits but also midnight showings of cult films. *The Rocky Horror Picture Show* played at midnight on Friday and Saturday nights for many years, and the theater allowed audience members to engage with the characters on screen by singing along, throwing toast or sporting umbrellas.

In the mall itself, between Sears on one end and J.C. Penney on the other, stores offered clothing for young people, snacks and fun and games. The Bottom Half, Check'rd Flag and Earring Tree offered fashion pieces, while Musicland sold record albums on vinyl that people could play on turntables. Radio Shack offered the latest tech items before they were referred to as "tech," while Orange Julius and Hot Sam's Soft Pretzels provided sustenance for those who weren't in the MCL Cafeteria demographic.

It's possible no storefront in Muncie Mall enjoyed as dedicated a clientele as Sultan's Castle, a pinball and video game arcade. In 1985, games like *Ms. Pac-Man*, *Donkey Kong Jr.* and *Dragon Slayer* were among the most popular. The latter, a fantasy adventure game, was popular with fans of Dungeons and Dragons, a role-playing game that counted Ethan Dixon among its fans.

16

THE TRAFFIC STOP

Although James "Jimmy" Swingley had left Muncie for Florida shortly after the Westside Park slayings—some people later told police investigators that he left town the day after—he had returned to Muncie by August 1986, when he had another encounter with local police.

On August 17, 1986, police pulled over the car Swingley was driving after he blew through a stop sign. When asked by the Muncie patrolman who stopped him, Swingley could not or would not produce his driver's license. Instead, he told the officer his name was Kevin Dixon—a last name shared by Ethan Dixon, who was shot to death in Westside Park eleven months earlier. Swingley also told the officer that he lived in Lakeland, Florida.

The traffic stop resulted in minor charges—no operator's license in possession and disregarding a stop sign—being filed in Delaware Superior Court 4 on November 26, 1986. Court records from 1991 indicate that Swingley had failed to appear for court hearings and did not pay the judgment and court costs stemming from the charge, so a default judgment was issued.

From the mid-1980s to the mid-1990s, Swingley had several brushes with the law. Court records show that he was charged with check deception, drunk driving, theft, burglary, intimidation, disorderly conduct and, on at least two occasions, public intoxication. Several of the charges were dismissed when Swingley agreed to plead guilty to another charge, conversion, in a 1996 theft case. He received a year of probation in that case and was ordered to stay away from his victim, a man named Roscoe Essex, who later played a role in Swingley's eventual prosecution and conviction on a murder charge. Until that murder case, Swingley's most high-profile offense was in connection with several burglaries that led to an aborted prosecution.

In 1985, Swingley, who was then twenty-two years old, was one of a dozen men charged with racketeering in connection with a series of business burglaries. The racketeering charge stemmed from the allegation that the men took part in a criminal organization that was created for the purpose of committing crimes—burglaries in Delaware and Randolph Counties in Indiana and two Ohio counties. The burglaries occurred between February and May 1984 and took place at three farm supply businesses, two drugstores and an electronics store.

Swingley and his codefendants were indicted by a Delaware Superior Court 1 grand jury. But an attorney acting for Swingley argued that his client was not guilty and that the Delaware County prosecutor's office had failed to provide evidence that he was involved in the crimes. After the prosecutor's office said that no additional information about Swingley was forthcoming, Judge Robert Barnet Jr. dismissed the racketeering charge.

Swingley's victory in court came on September 9, 1985, nineteen days before Kimberly Dowell and Ethan Dixon were shot to death in Westside Park.

Swingley next faced the most serious charge that can be levied against someone: murder.

MIDDLETOWN, THE TYPICAL SMALL AMERICAN CITY

While the Westside Park slayings were horrific, the public fascination outside the Muncie community afforded to the killings could probably be attributed to several factors, including Muncie's notoriety thanks to a 1920s sociological study that was taught in classrooms around the country for decades.

Middletown: A Study in Modern American Culture was published in 1929 by husband-and-wife sociologists Robert and Helen Lynd, based at Columbia University in New York. The study set out to paint a portrait of the typical small American city. The first study and a subsequent one, *Middletown in Transition* (1937), looked at the city—not identified as Muncie but dubbed Middletown—how its people lived, worked, worshipped and spent their free time and were governed.

The study, which has been updated several times—most notably in a 1982 PBS documentary series, *Middletown*, by documentarian Peter Davis—has been praised over the decades. But it has also been criticized because of the crucial parts of the community it either glossed over or ignored altogether—in particular, the African American population.

The Lynds, like later researchers who returned to Muncie to "check the temperature" of the community, conducted interviews, studied statistics and reviewed newspapers and historical documents.

The relationship between Muncie and the Middletown studies goes the other way, too—at least in terms of newspaper coverage over the decades that praised the studies, or at least the founding fathers of the city that was studied. In April 1937, the *Muncie Star* wrote about the Middletown studies, noting, "Lynd's candid approach to the Ball family [a family of industrialists who expanded a canning jar empire in Muncie] will warm the hearts of many readers who, for many years, have longed to shout instead of whisper when speaking of this family…[although] the working class, however, tends to resent the family and its power, while the business class favors them and covets their friendship.'" Lynd himself noted, "What does it do to a city full of people to live thus under the benevolent control of wealthy and influential related families?'"

The community was, perhaps like other cities of its size at the time, fairly narrow-minded. "Middletown occasionally tolerates a different personality, looking on him as a community pet, provided he does not have enough fellows to threaten the established order."

Locals sometimes rose to the defense of the community and its leaders in the wake of the studies, particularly the 1937 follow-up, which prompted Muncie pastor Hillyer Stratton of First Baptist Church to write a letter, denying that local residents thought of the Ball family as "an economic royalistic octopus, squeezing the life out of us poor devils in Muncie." As evidence of the community's admiration for the Balls, Stratton noted, ten thousand Muncie people had contributed $31,000 to construction of Beneficence, the memorial to the family's philanthropy that is located on the Ball State campus.

Muncie's reputation as a community that could serve as an avatar for American society continued throughout the decades. In December 1970, the *Muncie Star* reported that the *New York Times* sent a reporter, Alden Whitman, to Muncie for several days to observe and report on the community. "While Whitman was in town, he encountered, among others, a women's lib worker, a black minister, a relative of a 'founding father,' a sociologist and a factory worker." Whitman found what he called affection for the town on the part of its residents. Munsonians valued the same principals then as they had in the 1920s and 1930s, Whitman found. "Plenty of hard work and early hours." Whitman said nightlife in 1970 Muncie was "unexciting."

In 1977, a University of Virginia researcher who was updating the Middletown studies noted that a few things had changed in the forty years since the second Lynd study of the typical small American city. Among them, Muncie's divorce and death rates were higher than the national average.

In 1983, the episode "Seventeen" of the *Middletown* PBS series caused a furor over its cinéma vérité portrayal of Muncie high school students, including footage of bad student-teacher relationships, interracial dating, underage drinking and drug use and teen pregnancy—all punctuated with R-rated language. After the outcry, the episode didn't air as part of the regular series. "Seventeen" does have insight into the lives of teenagers in Muncie not long before the Westside Park slayings, but its frame of reference for the students at Southside High School spotlights a very different community than that of Northside High School, where Ethan Dixon and Kimberly Dowell attended.

It's unclear if the Middletown studies fueled the pop culture embrace of Muncie. Over the decades, Muncie has been the setting for or referenced by scenes, stories and characters in the *Tom Slick* Saturday morning cartoons of 1967; the movie *Close Encounters of the Third Kind*, which was directed by Steven Spielberg and released in 1977; the movie *The Hudsucker Proxy*, which was released in 1994 by directors Joel and Ethan Coen; the 2007 CBS reality TV series *Armed and Famous*, which put celebrities like Erik Estrada in the Muncie Police Department; and the fiction TV series *Angel* and *Agents of S.H.I.E.L.D.* Muncie's popular culture claims to fame include the city's status as the home of *Garfield* creator Jim Davis and where broadcaster David Letterman attended college at Ball State University. In recent years, Muncie became a running gag in the Indiana-set series *Parks and Recreation* because put-upon character Jerry in fictional Pawnee, Indiana, has a timeshare condo in Muncie.

POLITICAL PLAYERS IN MUNCIE

At the time of the Westside Park murders, Muncie politics was politically charged and full of colorful characters. This wasn't unusual for the town, as it was as infamous for its politics as its unsolved murders. What was unusual was the cast of characters in politics at the time. They were some of the most charismatic and, in some instances, controversial officeholders that Muncie and Delaware County had ever seen.

James Patrick Carey was the mayor of Muncie when Dixon and Dowell were killed, and he made personal pleas for information to help solve the case. As a matter of fact, Carey asked anyone with tips about the killings to contact him personally. That wasn't out of character for Carey, whose oversized personality made him one of the most distinctive characters in Muncie political history. Carey, a lifelong Democrat, joined the Muncie Police Department in 1949, after serving in the U.S Navy. He became the assistant chief in 1956 and was named chief in 1958.

Carey, beloved by many, was a controversial figure at times. In 1959, he was indicted by a grand jury based on allegations that he had allowed illegal gambling, liquor sales and prostitution to flourish in the city. The indictment was later dismissed. His political fortunes rose and fell depending on which party was in power, but he retired from the Muncie Police Department in 1970 and ran for the Delaware County sheriff seat, winning the office. In June 1972, Carey was arrested on bribery charges in connection with gambling activities. He was tried and found not guilty.

James P. Carey (*right*), the mayor of Muncie in 1985, being greeted by a supporter. *Author's collection.*

Carey ran for mayor of Muncie in 1979, losing to Republican Alan Wilson in a campaign that was documented in an episode of the PBS series *Middletown*. He was elected in 1983. He was reelected in 1987 but lost a bid for a third term in 1991 to Republican David Dominick, and he lost a 1995 campaign to Republican Dan Canan. He won a term on the Muncie City Council in 1999 before retiring in 2003. Carey died in October 2006.

Michael J. "Mick" Alexander was Delaware County's prosecuting attorney in September 1985, when Kimberly Dowell and Ethan Dixon were killed in the park. Alexander had been elected prosecutor in 1978 after a hard-fought war with his own party, the local Democrats. And after taking office, Alexander clashed with the Muncie Police Department. The mutual distrust was high, and the outspoken Alexander, who finished his second term as prosecutor and left office at the end of 1986, was not nearly as high-profile in the newspaper coverage of the murders of Dixon and Dowell as might have been expected. Alexander, who began his career as a state police officer before becoming an attorney, became a highly sought-after defense attorney after leaving office. He died in 2017.

Richard "Rick" Reed, Alexander's longtime friend and law partner, was elected prosecutor in 1990. Reed was a deputy prosecutor under Alexander at the time of the Westside Park shootings and was slightly more high-profile—but not much more. In a 2019 interview, Marvin Campbell, who was Muncie's deputy police chief in 1985, said he consulted with Reed in the early days of the investigation. Reed retired at the end of 2006.

Donald Scroggins was Muncie's police chief at the time of the killings, having been appointed by Mayor James P. Carey. Scroggins joined the Muncie Police Department in 1960 as a patrolman, serving later as the captain of detectives. He was named chief in 1983 and served in the position for the entirety of Carey's two terms. After leaving the city police department, he served as chief deputy sheriff and as an investigator in the prosecutor's office under Richard Reed. One Scroggins brother, Bobby, was a longtime Muncie firefighter, as was their brother, Glenn, who also served as the Delaware County coroner at the time of the Westside Park investigation. Scroggins's nephew Michael Scroggins, Glenn's son, was later the Delaware County sheriff.

Delaware County sheriff Gary Carmichael's department didn't participate in the Westside Park investigation, although it might have if a city–county homicide investigation team was still in place. But the joint investigative squad had been disbanded a few years earlier, and it was only reformed after the Westside murders. Carmichael, a Republican who appealed to so many Democratic Party voters that he was jokingly termed a "Republicrat," served two terms as sheriff—the state constitutional limit in Indiana—and left office at the end of 1986, when Glenn Scroggins ended his time as the coroner. Carmichael went on to serve as the county assessor before retiring. He died in February 2016.

19

A NICE PLACE

By the time of the September 1985 killings in Westside Park, the green space had existed in one form or another for more than one hundred years. Although research shows little hard-and-fast information about the opening date of the park, an early published reference came in the *Muncie Morning Star* in May 1894. "Westside Park is as nice a place as one could desire in which to while away these warm afternoons," read a paragraph in a column with local news. "The scenery adjacent the park is beautiful. Half a hundred or more benches have been provided by the street railway folks, and all can find a comfortable seat."

References to Westside Park most often noted that it was a western terminus for local interurban rail lines. The round trip cost ten cents, and the riders were encouraged by the local rail company, which owned and operated the park before the city took over in the mid-twentieth century.

In the spring of 1894, the newspaper noted that "thousands of people" were expected to watch a "Prof. Baldwin" undertake a balloon ascension and parachute jump. That kind of stunt—often including a trapeze act performed while hanging from a hot air balloon—was a common feature at the park.

Throughout the last several years of the nineteenth century, Westside was the scene of numerous gatherings for band concerts by traveling performers, as well as local churches and civic groups, who held their picnics in the park. The newspaper coverage of activities and incidents in the park was hyperbolic. In June 1895, the newspaper noted, "Mrs. Shepard of South Franklin Street visited Westside Park yesterday afternoon with three lady friends. They were walking about under the large shade trees when a big burly fellow, probably a tramp, insulted them by using some very impolite language. Mrs. Shepard told him to desist, or she would call the police, and the word 'police' had the desired effect, as the fellow left the park on the run." In August 1895, the "Westside Park police force" arrested a man for burglary. He was charged with stealing a cow and reselling it for $6.50.

In the early years of the twentieth century, an indoor roller-skating rink was one of the park's biggest draws. Work on the rink was to begin in 1899, although newspaper accounts indicated it didn't open until May 1908. "Westside Park will be the Mecca for pleasure-seeking visitors," a newspaper headline maintained. The article noted that the rink building measured nearly 800 feet in length and the rink itself was 585 feet in length.

Westside Park even inspired poetry. In the December 11, 1931 edition of the *Muncie Morning Star*, the poem "Westside Park" was published. "What grand adventure 'twas to ride—both child and patriarch—upon the trolley which brought up—in gladsome Westside Park....What glorious trees there used to be, what shadows cool and dark, for those who 'scaped from summer's heat, in grand old Westside Park." And so on, with references to the park's skating rink and swinging bridge. "We're glad we have McCulloch large and Heekin worth remark, but we can't help remember days in dear old Westside Park."

The park fell out of favor sometime in the first half of the twentieth century, however, and improvements were needed. In July 1953, the *Muncie Star* reported, "Westside Park Here to Be Revived." The park had been closed for more than thirty years, according to newspaper accounts.

The city parks board announced plans for reestablishing a new park; it was smaller than the original park at twelve acres. The land, now owned by the city, was bounded by the White River to the south, White River Boulevard to the north, Nichols Avenue to the east and Tillotson Avenue to the west. The parks board hoped to install a shelter house, restrooms and playground equipment by the summer of 1954. "The old Westside Park played an important part in the social life of Muncie in the early 1900s," the newspaper reported. "There was a well-patronized skating rink, beer garden, bandstand and a swinging bridge. Major social events were streetcar parties and outings to the park." In reviewing his administration's 1954 efforts, Mayor Joseph Barclay cited the redevelopment of Westside Park, replacing "an area that was once an eyesore."

The park saw renovations over the decades, most notably in new playground equipment and new recreational features, including tennis courts and basketball courts.

The roller-skating rink at Westside Park at the turn of the twentieth century. *Courtesy of Ball State University.*

In 1961, the *Muncie Star* reported, with the flavor of coverage of an ancient archaeological dig, the uncovering of the foundation of the long-gone roller-skating rink. Other features of Westside that had long since disappeared were a roller coaster and merry-go-round. By this point, a local JayCees group had established a baseball diamond at the park, and baseball and softball would soon be played before large crowds.

The city was cracking down on misuse of the park, proclaiming in 1961 a long list of items and activities that were not allowed, including open fires, dogs not on a leash, fireworks, BB guns, pea shooters, slingshots, water pistols and parking cars in areas that were not designated for parking. But the park also gained a reputation—as did other Muncie parks—as a place for young lovers to find a secluded spot.

In June 1983, a police officer surprised three people—all naked—in Westside. When he approached the group, one man, still sans clothing, quickly forded the White River and left the area. The remaining couple, including a seventeen-year-old girl, told the cop that they were parked when a man approached them, held them at gunpoint, made them get out of their car and then raped the girl.

LOVERS' LANE MURDERS

The Westside Park killings were tagged as a "lovers' lane" crime in the supermarket tabloid the *Weekly World News*, which more often "reported" on "news" involving aliens, Elvis and JFK The *Muncie Evening Press* reported that the Dixon and Dowell killings were featured in the November 12, 1985 edition of the tabloid under the headline "Lovers' Lane Murders." Such killings are often called "lovers' lane murders" because they involved a couple parked in a remote spot. But sometimes, any crime against a couple—or even just two victims—was similarly described.

The most notorious "lovers' lane" killer may be David Berkowitz, the so-called Son of Sam killer, who was arrested in 1977 and charged with committing eight shooting attacks in New York City, which began in 1976 and left six people dead and seven wounded. Berkowitz targeted, for the most part, people who were sitting in parked cars on New York streets.

Also famous but still unsolved were the Zodiac killings in the late 1960s and 1970s in the greater San Francisco area. In one instance, the Zodiac stabbed two college students in a rural location, leaving one dead and one seriously injured.

In November 1977, two teenagers were abducted from a New Orleans– area "lovers' lane" and shot to death by Patrick Sonnier, who, in April 1984, was executed via electric chair by the State of Louisiana.

Sometimes, lovers' lane murders are turned into mass-market entertainment. The 1977 film *The Town That Dreaded Sundown* was purported to be based on a true story of a series of lovers' lane killings in Texarkana, Texas, in 1948. That crime spree was never solved, according to the film.

Sometimes, justice is slow in coming but finally arrives. In March 1963, police in San Luis Obispo, California, charged a man, Gale Patrick Irish, with the murders of three people in a series of crimes that dated as far back as 1950. Irish, who was already in prison on unrelated charges at the time he signed a confession, confessed to crimes that included walking up on a couple parked on a lovers' lane and shooting the man in the head. The woman in the car was initially taken prisoner by Irish but escaped.

A notorious Kansas crime occurred in 1982, when two teenagers in Independence, Kansas, were shot multiple times and killed. But while the "why" behind the slayings was a mystery, the assailant was apparently not, as a third teenager was arrested immediately.

One of the strangest cases of multiple murders—sometimes referred to as a lovers' lane case—led to an arrest, long imprisonment and eventual release in an Indiana story that made headlines over a three-decade period. In 1947, Ralph Lobaugh was sentenced to die in Indiana's electric chair after confessing to raping and killing three women in the Fort Wayne area. The murders took place over a series of several months in 1944; the victims were Wilhemena "Billy" Haaga, a thirty-eight-year-old described as "an attractive blond war worker"; Ann or Anna Kuseff, a nineteen-year-old who also worked in a defense plant; and Phyllis Conine, a seventeen-year-old high school student. Killed at about the same time was Dorothea Howard, an army wife. The killings terrified Fort Wayne residents in the waning days of World War II. Lobaugh went to Kokomo police in June 1947 and confessed to killing Haaga and Kuseff, but he got the victims' names and sequence of the killings wrong.

As later newspaper accounts reported, the Fort Wayne killings had enflamed the city election there and turned it into a referendum on city leadership and the police. Lobaugh was transported to Fort Wayne, where he additionally confessed to killing Howard but not Conine, whose murder had previously been cited along with Haaga and Kuseff's killings as perhaps the work of the same serial murderer. In most of the cases, the victim had been accosted and killed while outdoors, sometimes in a remote place, and their body likewise left outside.

Lobaugh pleaded guilty to three murders and was sentenced to Indiana's death row in February 1948. However, following Lobaugh's sentencing, Fort Wayne police arrested another man, Robert Christen, for killing Howard, and in August 1949, they arrested Franklin Click for raping a local woman. While he was being interrogated, Click confessed to killing Haaga, Kuseff and Conine. After the trials of Christen and Click, Indiana had three men in prison for the same set of murders.

At the request of Governor Henry Schricker, an investigation was conducted that led to the conclusion that, while Lobaugh should remain in prison—he had been described as a "high school dropout, menial laborer and an erratic, mixed-up oddball with a failing marriage, sex hang-ups and a drinking problem"—he wasn't guilty of murder. The governor commuted Lobaugh's sentence from death to life in prison.

In 1950, the Indiana Supreme Court overturned Christen's conviction, and he was freed. Later that year, Click died in the electric chair.

In the spring of 1977, Lobaugh, who was then sixty, was released from prison when Governor Otis Bowen approved his clemency. By October 1977, Lobaugh had asked for—and was granted—permission to return to prison, saying he could no longer stand to be free.

Newspaper records don't indicate any resolution to the question of who killed Dorothea Howard or if, indeed, justice had been served in the other slayings.

THE CONCORDIA, KANSAS MURDERS

Confronted with a lack of leads in the Westside Park murders, Muncie police investigators began to look elsewhere, even across the country, for similar crimes that might have proven fruitful to their investigation of the killings of Kimberly Dowell and Ethan Dixon. *Could the killer of Dixon and Dowell have been responsible for similar slayings elsewhere?*

In the weeks following the Westside crimes, deputy police chief Marvin Campbell told newspaper reporters that investigators looked at "similar" killings in Concordia, Kansas. In a 2019 interview, Campbell said he recalled that local investigators looked at crimes elsewhere, but he couldn't remember any details.

The case that local investigators looked at, from a distance, was the October 1980 slayings of Shaun Champlin and Tina Montoy. Champlin, who was eighteen years old, and Montoy, who was twenty, had been dating for about a year. He had played high school football and was a student at Cloud County Community College. She had graduated from the community college and worked as a teacher's aide. They talked about going to college together in Topeka. Like Dixon and Dowell, the two were considered model young citizens. Montoy had made headlines before, in 1978, when she was eighteen and named the Kansas GI Forum Queen. When Champlin made the newspaper, it had been for his football prowess.

The two went to their school's homecoming dance on October 19, 1980, and were last seen at the festivity. But their bodies were later found in Champlin's Chevrolet Monte Carlo in a wooded area near Concordia, a town of about six thousand people. Montoy had been shot in the head, and Champlin had been shot in the shoulder, back and leg. A passing motorist, who had pulled off the road in the area, found the car with Champlin and Montoy's nude bodies. Champlin's car was found along what was described as a "tree-shrouded, one-lane" road that was known as a "lovers' lane."

By December 1980, a reward for information leading to the arrest of Champlin and Montoy's killer amounted to $15,000. Residents of the town, especially young people, said they feared for their lives and had stopped going out at night. One eighteen-year-old Concordia woman said that more people had begun carrying loaded guns. The Cloud County Sheriff's Office said that investigators had spent more than eight hundred hours on the case in an effort to find the couple's killer. "We just ran out of leads and came to a dead end," retired sheriff Fred Modlin said.

In January 1982, Concordia police said they had focused on a new, previously overlooked suspect in the killings, but police didn't name the person of interest. Police said they were looking at a "kook or a psychotic" in the killings. "What you're looking for is a kook, or a psychotic, who just happened to go to this place and commit this act," Concordia police chief Dennis Rohr said. "In my mind, I don't feel they were singled out. Anyone who was out there could have been a victim."

The prevailing police theory in Kansas was definitely different from that in Muncie, where police focused on Kimberly Dowell's stepfather. In July 1984, Kansas authorities said they wanted to speak to Steven Carl Holdren, who had been found not guilty in the 1977 murder of a Belleville, Kansas woman, around the time of the killings of Champlin and Montoy. A newspaper article cited several open cases, including that of a woman missing from Hays, Kansas, that Holdren might have had to answer to. But ultimately, Holdren, in 1986, pleaded guilty to aggravated kidnapping in a case unrelated to the slayings of Champlin and Montoy.

In 2001, the Kansas Bureau of Investigation took on the case. The KBI Cold Crime Squad announced that it would look into the crime, which had been committed twenty-one years earlier. News coverage of the announcement prompted several phone calls from people who were offering information about the crime. But a 2003 article in the *Salina* (KS) *Journal* noted that the killings of Champlin and Montoy remained unsolved and that no suspect had been arrested and charged.

Montoy's father, Oswald, went to his grave knowing that his daughter's killer was never found. He died in 2001 at the age of seventy-two.

22

THE FRIEND, RAMBO AND OTHER THEORIES

Amy Leffingwell remembers when her friend went off the rails: right after the murders of Kimberly Dowell and Ethan Dixon. Leffingwell—like Ethan, a Northside High School class officer—had been part of a circle of friends that included Joseph [a pseudonym]. Joseph was an amiable kid, Leffingwell said, who seemed more than unsettled by the killings of their classmates. He seemed seriously unbalanced by it.

Leffingwell remembered how Joseph became obsessed with the killings. She remembered how he came to her house one night and tapped on her window, seeking entry. She remembered that he had even told their small circle of friends that he had a knife—that he could kill all of them and no one could stop him.

Joseph went into the military not long after graduating from Northside High School, and Leffingwell lost track of him. Years later, she determined that he was living in a Muncie housing project for the indigent. Leffingwell wondered for decades if Joseph had some role in the slayings of Ethan and Kimberly, or if that tragedy was what pushed him over the edge somehow.

Joseph was not the first person who seemed affected—or even threatening—in the wake of the killings. Leffingwell kept her suspicions to herself. Others did not. Accounts of suspicious activity and rumors of guilt continued over the decades and were recounted to latter-day police investigators. Most were vague suspicions that couldn't be followed up on. Others prompted thorough checking.

In 2012, Muncie police spoke to a man who recalled hearing relatives talk about "helping" a man after the murders.

In 2013, a retired Delaware County police officer told Muncie police investigators that he had been told that the son of a prominent local person was involved in the slayings and that he had driven a car to northern Indiana to dispose of it shortly afterward.

In September 2014, the authors of this book published a story in the *Star Press* newspaper about the case, the renewed investigation by the Muncie Police Department and, particularly, the work of MPD investigator Nathan Sloan. In the days and weeks that followed the article's publication, people came out of the woodwork with theories and suspects.

A county police officer who would later have his own troubles with the law (he was arrested for stealing Delaware County police ammunition and reselling it) contacted MPD and singled out the small-town police officer who had been in Westside Park the night of the Dixon and Dowell homicides.

A Delaware County Jail inmate fingered the son of a prominent political family, who reportedly drove a Monte Carlo in September 1985. The inmate said he was on hand when the son, while getting high near Prairie Creek Reservoir, reportedly admitted his involvement.

A man told police that the composite drawing of a suspect that had been released by police back in 1985 and reprinted in the *Star Press* in September 2014 "looked like" a man he knew, although he had no information that actually connected the man to the crime.

A woman recalled that on the night of the slayings, a friend of the son of her "gentleman friend" came running into their house and said he had done a "bad thing." The woman said that neither she nor her gentleman friend knew the name of the friend.

A man recalled that on the night of the killings, a guest had left a party but then returned "dressed like Rambo" with a "wild look" in his eyes. The would-be Rambo had experience with drugs but not guns, the caller said, but he didn't have any evidence to connect him to the park slayings.

And a man came forward to accuse a woman of the killings, saying he believed that the woman had mistakenly killed Ethan and Kimberly when she thought she had caught him in a parked car with another woman.

23

THE YEAR FOLLOWING WESTSIDE

As 1986 opened, Muncie police were no closer to making an arrest of those responsible for killing Ethan Dixon and Kimberly Dowell than they had been at any time in the three months after their deaths. On January 27, deputy police chief Marvin Campbell told the *Muncie Evening Press* that he would seek a formal coroner's inquiry in the case. But Delaware County coroner Glenn Scroggins said that he had already conducted his office's inquiry. "In order for me to arrange for a formal inquiry, I need probable cause to cause me to believe that additional information or evidence could be obtained through that process," Scroggins said.

The newspaper explained that, in a coroner's inquiry, witnesses are subpoenaed, and testimony is taken under oath, with the penalty of perjury possible. Scroggins noted that, while Campbell had asked him about the coroner's inquiry, he had received no formal request to conduct one.

Campbell also said it was possible police would ask county prosecutor Michael J. "Mick" Alexander to conduct a grand jury investigation into the crime.

There's no indication from newspaper coverage that a coroner's inquiry or a grand jury investigation was ever conducted in the Westside Park case. In fact, on January 30, 1986, Scroggins—who left his office at the end of the year—said he did not intend to conduct a coroner's inquiry. Scroggins noted that he had determined the cause of death of the teenagers and said he would not reopen his investigation in lieu of additional information. "I have fulfilled my responsibility," Scroggins said.

Campbell later said that he had withdrawn his request for a coroner's inquiry, adding that it was "no big deal" that Scroggins had declined to conduct such an investigation.

At the four-month mark after the killings—mistakenly referred to as the five-month mark in the January 27 *Evening Press* article—Campbell also said that police had met with the families of Ethan and Kimberly, although the deputy chief said that one parent had sent a letter saying they would not attend. He did not publicly identify the parent. The meeting with the Dixon and Dowell parents was done to bring them up to date on the investigation.

The reward for anyone who provided information to solve the crime had topped $22,000 by the end of January 1986.

By the end of 1986, Muncie and Delaware County officials had agreed to once again cooperate in investigating local homicides like the Westside Park case, which was likely to benefit from such cooperation.

In December 1986, Delaware county sheriff-elect Dan Elliott, who followed Gary Carmichael in the county police department's top position, gathered with other incoming officials—Prosecutor Raymond Brassart, who followed Michael J. "Mick" Alexander; Coroner Jack Stonebraker Jr., who followed Glenn Scroggins; and Muncie police chief Donald Scroggins—to announce the return of the city–county homicide investigations team. Stonebraker, an ally of outgoing coroner Glenn Scroggins, led the team. The members of the team were tapped based on their skills and expertise. The team drew members from the city and county police departments, as well as from six Delaware County towns and the Ball State University police department.

A previous joint city–county homicide team had been formed in 1980, but it was disbanded within two years, reportedly as a result of a political feud between then-prosecutor Alexander and then-mayor Alan Wilson. But in 1983, political fortunes realigned, and Wilson lost a reelection bid to James P. Carey.

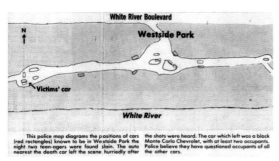

A map of Westside Park published in the *Muncie Evening Press* on October 8, 1985, showing the approximate locations of the vehicles in the park the night Ethan Dixon and Kimberly Dowell were killed. *Courtesy of Muncie Newspapers.*

Northside, the "preppy" school that was populated to a great extent by Muncie's privileged children, saw more violence and tragedy before 1986 was done. In March 1986, one student stabbed another when a scuffle broke out after "roughhousing got out of hand and turned to violence." The seventeen-year-old victim's wound was not life-threatening. The year closed with another note of tragedy and violent death for the careworn students of the school. In December, Thomas Dunlap Jr., a Northside High School senior, died of a gunshot wound to the head from his own muzzle-loader rifle, according to news accounts. The seventeen-year-old was hunting deer with family members in LaGrange County when the accident occurred. Authorities said he was alone and walking on a fallen log when he fell, causing his gun to discharge. Relatives found his body.

Unlike the families of Ethan Dixon and Kimberly Dowell, who lived in some of Muncie's more prestigious neighborhoods, Dunlap's family lived in a northside neighborhood, Morningside, that was often seen as working class. The nature of Dunlap's death, while violent, was admittedly not mysterious, and the headlines about his death were small and few and far between.

In a letter to the editor of the local newspapers, the Dunlaps' neighbor Ervin Davis recalled the young man as someone whose "smile would transform a dark room into light and joy in an instant, and his kind nature warmed the hearts of everyone he met."

TRAGEDY AND THE WINTERS BROTHERS

When Muncie police patrolman Terry Winters found the bodies of Kimberly Dowell and Ethan Dixon in Ethan's car in Westside Park on September 28, 1985, he made a discovery that had an impact on the rest of his life. It also marked him as a suspect in the minds of a few people—even to this day.

It was not Winters's only brush with sudden, tragic death. His brother, who was also a police officer, died from a gunshot wound just five years later.

In a September 2014 interview with the *Star Press*, Terry Winters recalled how shocked he was when he heard, not long after the killings of Dixon and Dowell, that some people believed he was the killer. "It bothered me very much," Winters said, blaming the rumor on erroneous reports that were circulated that said he was off duty and just happened to be walking his dog in the park when he found the slain teenagers. Winters was walking his canine partner, but he was also telling people to leave the park after it closed at 11:00 p.m., which was part of his duties.

Winters recalled in 2014 that calls to the office of Mayor James Carey prompted Muncie Police Department leadership to order him to surrender his guns for testing to see if they were used in the crime. "I was stunned. I was just doing my job," Winters said. "It was bad enough just coming upon that situation." Testing showed that Winters's weapons had not been used in the killings of Dixon and Dowell. However, the rumor persisted.

"Who did it? I probably thought the police officer did it," Ethan's classmate Julie Davey said in a 2019 interview. "He was there so quickly."

Davey acknowledged that she didn't have a hard-and-fast theory and noted that Kim's stepfather was on the scene quickly, too. "To this day, I still think it was the police officer or her stepdad [who] had something to do with it," Davey added.

Winters was unfairly tarnished to some because of the stories that circulated that he was off duty at the time—as if anyone, civilian or off-duty police officer, could not have come upon the two dead teenagers that night.

Winters's life was again marred by tragedy just five years and three months later. In the early morning hours of December 28, 1990, Delaware County police officer Gregg Winters was transporting Michael A. Lambert, who had been arrested for public intoxication, to the county jail on Riggin Road on Muncie's north side. The building, a former warehouse, was Delaware County's temporary jail when a new building, the county Justice Center, was being built downtown. But something went horribly wrong in Lambert's arrest and the moments that followed. Lambert had concealed a gun on his body and, in spite of the handcuffs he wore, pulled the gun out and fired five times into the back of Gregg Winters's head. The thirty-two-year-old officer never recovered. He died on January 8, 1991, having never awakened.

Police believed that Lambert, who was twenty years old, had stolen the handgun he used to kill Gregg Winters from his employer a few days before. He had the gun hidden in the back of his pants or in a shoe when he was placed in Winters's police car.

Terry Winters was getting ready for bed when a police dispatcher called to tell him his brother had been shot. "I asked, 'What do you mean he's been shot?'" Winters told the *Star Press* newspaper in 2003. "'Is he still alive?' They told me he was still alive, but it didn't look good."

A jury took less than two hours to find Lambert guilty of the murder of Gregg Winters. In January 1992, Delaware Superior Court 1 judge Robert Barnet Jr. imposed the death penalty on Lambert. It was only the second such sentence handed down in Delaware County history. Michael Lambert was executed by lethal injection at the Indiana State Prison in Michigan City in June 2007.

Gregg Winters's widow went on to become an advocate for the survivors of other police officers killed in the line of duty. Molly and Gregg Winters's two sons grew up without their father. The boys were only three years old and ten months old when their father was killed.

A month before his brother's killer was executed, Terry Winters—who was a witness at Lambert's execution—told the *Star Press*, "I'll always

Terry Winters in the late 1980s, by which point he was an investigator with the Muncie Police Department. *Author's collection.*

grieve the loss of my brother." Terry Winters was the deputy police chief in Muncie in 2003. He retired a decade later but came back to the department as a reserve officer. Reflecting on a career and life marked by tragedy, he told the *Star Press*, "I never thought about giving up and quitting this job. I know Gregg wouldn't want that."

ANNIVERSARIES OF THE CASE

A year after the murders, the Westside Park case was called "the most extensive and intense investigation" in recent memory by the *Muncie Evening Press*.

As the end of September 1986 rolled around, thoughts were turned to the slayings of Kimberly Dowell and Ethan Dixon, which had occurred a year earlier. Muncie police were still investigating the case, police chief Don Scroggins said, but he added, "We've done everything we could think of to do."

Marvin Campbell, the deputy chief, said the department still received tips and kept in contact with other police departments about homicides that seemed similar. Early rumors took "many man hours" to follow up on, Scroggins said, and the circumstances of the killings presented no "obvious motive." Both the chief and deputy chief did say, however, that they believed the killings of Dixon and Dowell were selective and not random.

Campbell said he still had the same suspect in mind as a year earlier: Kimberly's stepfather, Donald Vogelgesang, although the man's name is not mentioned in the article, which was written by reporter Joe Canan. Campbell said the suspect, Don, was still under consideration because, after "inconclusive" results of a lie detector test, the person had refused to further cooperate with the department's investigation.

Perhaps for the first time, Campbell revealed that police had consulted with a psychic. In a 2019 interview, Campbell said that the psychic had led them to suspect the owner of a prominent Muncie restaurant. No arrest followed that theory, however.

An aerial view of a portion of Muncie, Indiana, with Westside Park near the bottom of the image. Rings for flying model airplanes are visible in the lower left corner, and the drive along the river, where the bodies of Ethan Dixon and Kimberly Dowell were found, is visible. *Courtesy of Ball State University.*

The police officials also acknowledged that the case had been turned over to subsequent investigators, who took a look at it with fresh eyes. Campbell said he was confident the crime would be solved. "Someone's living with that, and I can't imagine anyone being cold enough that this homicide hasn't taken a toll on their conscience."

Subsequent anniversaries did not pass without notice by police or newspapers. On the tenth anniversary of the murders, a police stakeout was held in Westside Park. In a 2010 article by the authors of this book in the *Star Press* newspaper, former Muncie deputy police chief Robert Weller said that he sent officers to the park just before midnight on September 28, 1995.

"We staked out the park the night of the tenth anniversary on the off chance the killer would come back," Weller said. "We were in that park until dawn." On that tenth anniversary, the *Muncie Star* and the *Muncie Evening Press* did retrospective articles on the killings. Police acknowledged that they hadn't received any new information since the year before.

In September 1997, on the twelfth anniversary of the killings, the authors of this book wrote an article for the *Star Press* newspaper that detailed, for the first time, some of the thoughts of Vogelgesang. (These were excerpted in an earlier chapter of this book.)

It would be a 2010 newspaper article, written by the authors of this book on the twenty-fifth anniversary of the murders, that not only renewed police scrutiny of the case but also led, over the course of years, one investigator to focus his work on a man who was often cited by associates and friends as being in connection with the murders of Dixon and Dowell: James "Jimmy" Swingley.

26

THROUGH FRESH EYES

As the years following the Westside Park killings of Kimberly Dowell and Ethan Dixon stretched on, the Muncie Police Department returned to the case again and again, assigning, variously, some veteran and young and promising detectives to dig through file boxes of notes and witness statements from the case. The idea was that "fresh eyes" would help the new detectives notice something that the previous investigators had not.

In February 2012, those "fresh eyes" belonged to Nathan Sloan, a Muncie police detective who spent a good part of the next several years not only looking at the old files but also interviewing—in some cases, interviewing again—potential witnesses, family members, suspects and people with information.

One of Sloan's first actions, after spending what he called two weeks "locked in a room" and reviewing the files, was to meet with a Muncie man and his attorney in a downtown law office. The man said he believed a couple, a man and a woman, may have been responsible for the killings. The man said the two were in a van in the park the night of the slayings. Sloan later said he found the information to be "mediocre at best," but it was entered into the official supplemental report on the Westside Park killings. Almost nothing was totally disregarded in the years that followed.

Sloan reviewed reports and interviews dating back to the 1980s, scanned court cases from the previous two decades and fielded calls from the public, would-be informants and his fellow police officers. He and other Muncie officers conducted new interviews with people who had already spoken to police, as well as those who had never been interviewed before.

Within weeks of the killings, people began telling police that they believed James "Jimmy" Swingley was, at the very least, involved in the murders of Dixon and Dowell.

On October 5, 1985, a man whose house was broken into—just a few houses down a westside Muncie street from where Swingley lived—said he believed Swingley had committed the burglary. The man told two police officers that he believed Swingley was involved in or had some knowledge of the Westside Park killings. In early December 1985—around the same time Swingley was arrested in Florida for holding a knife to a man's throat and threatening him over his comment that Swingley didn't have "the balls" to go to Australia—Muncie police officers began talking about Swingley as a possible suspect.

At this time, police interviewed Swingley's girlfriend, whom he later married, at the criminal investigations division office at Muncie City Hall. It's unknown what, if anything, happened as a result.

In 1986, police continued to hear about Swingley and his possible involvement, until August 17, 1986, when Swingley was pulled over by Muncie police and gave his name as "Kevin Dixon."

A milestone of the investigation, which dated back decades but had largely been taken for granted by earlier investigators, caught Sloan's attention. On September 16, 1987—less than two years after the killings—Jimmy Swingley was given a PSE, or psychological stress evaluator test, by Muncie police. Sloan said in a 2019 interview that Swingley had failed three relevant questions on what is commonly referred to as a lie detector test. All three questions that Swingley failed addressed the shootings in Westside Park.

27

THE RAILROAD KILLER

Muncie is crisscrossed by railroad tracks. In the city's industrial heyday, the tracks serviced factories and other industries that made the city hum. By the 1980s, however, the tracks and the trains that still run on them, which were operated by CSX Transportation and Norfolk Southern Railway, were mostly seen as a nuisance, stopping cars that were trying to move along thoroughfares like Tillotson Avenue and Memorial Drive. *But could the tracks have enabled a serial killer, one that might even have killed Ethan Dixon and Kimberly Dowell, to visit Muncie?*

In 2013, Muncie police investigator Nathan Sloan was talking to someone close to the victims when the person mentioned Ángel Maturino Reséndiz, who was also dubbed the "Railroad Killer," the "Railway Killer" and the "Railcar Killer." *Could Reséndiz have used the railroad tracks near Westside Park to find two victims in September 1985?*

Reséndiz, who was born in Mexico in 1959, was executed in Texas in 2006. He was a suspect in the killings of twenty-three people but was formally connected to fifteen killings. The earliest known to the authorities were those of two people—names unknown, but they were boyfriend and girlfriend—who were killed in Texas in 1986. At least one of those two victims was apparently shot with a .38-caliber handgun. Reséndiz confessed to these crimes in 2001.

But Reséndiz's method of murder was generally to bludgeon or strangle his victims. His list of identified crimes began in 1991 and ran through 1999. His crimes were known to have occurred in Texas, Georgia, Florida,

A railroad car sits on a siding in Muncie, Indiana. *Courtesy of Ball State University.*

California and as far north as the town of Gorham, Illinois, and the city of Lexington, Kentucky. In the Kentucky case, Reséndiz killed Christopher Maier, a University of Kentucky student who had been walking along some Lexington railroad tracks in August 1997. Reséndiz bludgeoned Maier with a large rock and raped and beat Maier's girlfriend, Holly Dunn Pendleton, who was the only person known to have survived an attack by Reséndiz. Pendleton later founded Holly's House, a resource for victims, in her native Evansville, Indiana.

It was believed that Reséndiz would ride on freight cars to towns in several states, where he would hop off the train and commit murder before making his way out of the city or town. He was the subject of a manhunt and was on the FBI's list of most wanted fugitives before he surrendered to authorities in Texas in 1999. He was charged with the murder of Claudia Benton, a pediatric neurologist whom he killed at the Baylor College of Medicine in December 1998. His defense was that he was insane.

After he was found mentally competent to be executed in 2006, Reséndiz said, "I don't believe in death. I know the body is going to go to waste. But me, as a person, I'm eternal. I'm going to live forever." Reséndiz also claimed he was "half man and half angel" and could not be killed. He was put to death by means of lethal injection by the State of Texas in June 2006.

In a 2003 interview, Reséndiz said he had committed many more murders than those that had been attributed to him and that innocent people were in jail for his killings.

After Reséndiz's name was mentioned to Sloan, the investigator began researching the killer to see if he could have been responsible for the killings of Ethan and Kimberly. Westside Park is near railroad tracks on its north and south sides. The nearest track is as close as six hundred feet to the park. However, Sloan concluded that the theory that Reséndiz had killed in Muncie was "unlikely" but acknowledged that the killer's methods fit the time period and geographical area, as well as, loosely, the facts of the case.

In the wake of his execution, Reséndiz's role in other cases will never be known.

28

"YOU KNOW WHAT FOR"

Over the course of thirty-five years after the killings of Ethan Dixon and Kimberly Dowell in Westside Park, Muncie police investigators found themselves with incidents and tips that led to credible suspects—at least they seemed credible at the time.

After midnight on September 30, 1985—less than forty-eight hours after the killings—two Muncie police officers noticed a car, headlights off, parked on a small gravel road in Westside Park. As the officers' car approached, the parked car started up and moved toward them. The patrol car blocked the vehicle so it couldn't leave, and the officers approached the car. Inside, they found a man—called Andrew Able here to preserve his anonymity—who was intoxicated. His pants were soiled, and he said he was "grieving." Able told the officers, "You know what for." He was arrested for driving under the influence. The next day, he told detectives that he had been drinking and was simply sad because of the killings.

Able had lived in several cities in Texas, Arkansas and California. Police also found that Able had lived in the Kansas City area, not far from Concordia, Kansas, the scene of the shooting deaths of a young couple parked in a car, as recounted in an earlier chapter in this book.

In 2012, following up on old leads, Muncie police investigator Nathan Sloan talked to Able's ex-wife, who said that Able was an alcoholic who was prone to blackouts. She said that when they were married, he would get out of bed at night and leave their house without her knowledge. He had done that the night police stopped him in Westside Park, she said. The ex-wife said that, at the time, she had wondered if her then-husband had something to do with the killings but dismissed the idea.

Sloan later learned that Able had a criminal record for burglaries in California. In 1976, Able—still a teenager and identified in newspapers as a transient—was arrested for break-ins at a school and a home. He was convicted of "prowling" and sentenced to six months in the county jail. Able's ex-wife remembered that, around 1981, they were driving around a rural area near a small town not far from Kansas City when they were pulled over by police. They were questioned but ultimately released. The killings of Shaun Champlin and Tina Montoy occurred in October 1980 in Concordia, Kansas, three hours from Kansas City.

In the early 1990s, veteran police investigators Steve Stanley and Paul Cox spoke to Steve Tanner—his real name—an inmate at the Indiana Reformatory in Pendleton. Tanner was serving a twenty-year sentence for armed robbery, and he told Stanley and Cox the name of a suspect in the killings of Dixon and Dowell. Tanner said the murder was the result of a drug deal gone bad; the men who gathered in the park for a marijuana sale saw it fall through, spotted the teenagers and took their frustrations out by shooting them. But as Stanley and Cox acknowledged after interviewing another person in a small town in Virginia, the story ultimately didn't check

Westside Park in 2019. *Courtesy of Jordan Kartholl.*

out. For one thing, Tanner had claimed Dixon and Dowell were shot with a shotgun, and that wasn't the case. The investigators ultimately believed that Tanner had made up the story in an effort to get out of prison.

Around July 1991, police heard from a man who said his mother's ex-husband, Barry Baker (a pseudonym), and an associate were responsible for the murders. Sloan looked at the report again in 2013 and interviewed the woman, who said that Baker was capable of the killings. Baker worked for a large Muncie employer and, within a month of the killings, had been fired after a theft that his employers believed was related to substance abuse. He was also known to carry a .38-caliber handgun. Baker was deceased by the time Sloan began reviewing allegations against him and interviewing people who knew him.

Sometimes, the police received tips about multiple suspects in the Westside Park killings. Some of those led to James "Jimmy" Swingley.

29

THE GROUP

I n the late 1980s and into the 1990s, a small group of associates—some of whom were convicted of crimes and knew James "Jimmy" Swingley—operated in the underbelly of Muncie. At one time or another, some members of the group implicated others in the Westside Park killings. While some of the group members' activities were known to police investigators in the months and years following the deaths of Kimberly Dowell and Ethan Dixon, Muncie police detective Nathan Sloan started charting the past activities of the group after 2012, when he was assigned by his superiors in the department to review the case.

In January 1986, just four months after the slayings, county police officer Steve Aul, who became the Delaware County sheriff a few years later, talked to a man who told him that Swingley was afraid police would look for him in connection with the Dixon and Dowell murders.

A police investigator—not from Muncie's police department—was told in February 1987 by a man close to Swingley that Swingley came to his house the night of the homicides and said that he had been with two other people in Westside Park that night. A drug deal had gone bad, Swingley told the man, and teenagers in a parked car had been killed. Swingley told the man that one of the three men had pulled a gun and the holster had come out with it. (This lined up with the holster that was found in Ethan Dixon's car, but that information had been reported in local newspapers, so the anecdote could have been made up to fit the facts of the case.)

Another man, who died in the early 1990s, had worked on the "kill line" at the Marhoefer Meat Packing Plant and was the subject of some information given to Sloan in 2012. Police were told that the man was a drug dealer and was violent. Among his associates was Jimmy Swingley. Around the time of the murders, the man drove a Chevrolet Monte Carlo, a vehicle that had been sought by police since that night in Westside Park. The man also lived near the park.

Steven Tanner, who was cited in an earlier chapter about a report that police eventually decided didn't check out, was part of a group of four people who, police were told, were present when Dixon and Dowell were killed. Tanner had told police that one of the members of his circle had shot the teenagers, but some investigators dismissed the story because he claimed a shotgun was used. But when Sloan was reviewing the case in the 2010s, he found that police were told that one member of the group also had a .38-caliber handgun—like the weapon that had been used to kill the Northside students.

At some point in the years following the murders, a person close to one of the victims said she knew Tanner and thought he was capable of the crime. In 2013, Sloan talked to a woman who said that Tanner had told her the story of what happened in the park that night long before he first told police. Sloan also spoke with Tanner himself in 2013. The man acknowledged that the tale he told Muncie detectives in the early 1990s was fiction. Tanner even gave Sloan his own theory about who had committed the crime. It was a theory that ultimately resulted in further investigations but no arrests.

30

THE MURDER OF BRIAN INSCO

leven years and a few weeks after Kimberly Dowell and Ethan Dixon were killed in Westside Park, another killing made Muncie headlines. The resulting legal case wouldn't be resolved for more than two years and would mean a lengthy prison sentence for James "Jimmy" Swingley.

Brian Insco, who was thirty-two years old, was found nearly decapitated in his North Monroe Street apartment on November 11, 1996. Nineteen-year-old James Essex called 9-1-1 after he found his roommate, Insco, dead. Insco was on his bed with a pillow over his face. Police found a knife nearby, and in the apartment of his neighbor Roscoe "Rocky" Essex, James Essex's father, they found a wallet insert they believed belonged to Insco. Police came to believe that James Essex had beaten Insco in the head and stomach with a shovel and then Swingley cut Insco's throat. Rocky Essex told police a year later that he saw Swingley cut Insco's throat, and James Essex worked out a deal with prosecutors that he would not be charged in connection with the murder in exchange for his testimony against Swingley. The dispute that led to Insco's death was over forty-seven dollars that Insco owed toward the rent on the apartment.

In 1997, a woman close to Swingley told police that he had dropped the knife he used to kill Swingley down a storm drain. Another woman told police that Swingley said he cut Insco's throat to "put him out of his misery." A pathologist who examined Insco said his head was "mostly severed" from his body. Insco died of exsanguination, or severe blood loss, from cuts to his carotid artery and jugular vein.

On May 22, 1998, a Delaware County grand jury indicted the thirty-five-year-old Swingley on a murder charge in connection to Insco's death. The indictment followed two days of testimony in front of the grand jury. Authorities said Swingley had been charged with intimidation several months earlier as a result of an encounter with a man—described as an "eyewitness" to the killing of Insco—in which Swingley was alleged to have told the man to keep his mouth shut if "he wanted to keep on living."

The prosecutor in the case called Insco's killing "about as brutal a murder as you'll find in Delaware County," noting that Swingley had "practically cut his head off." Swingley's defense attorney said that Insco's roommate, James Essex, and Essex's father, Rocky, had actually committed the crime. On February 18, 1999, a Delaware Circuit Court jury deliberated for less than four hours before finding Swingley guilty of murdering Insco. Brian Insco's mother, Ann Hinshaw, expressed relief when Swingley was convicted. "I wanted justice for him," she said. In April 1999, Delaware Circuit Court judge Steven Caldemeyer sentenced Swingley to the maximum prison sentence, sixty-five years.

Swingley maintained his innocence. "I didn't do it," he told Caldemeyer. "The dude who did it walked out of the courtroom free." Swingley was referring to James Lee Essex, Insco's roommate, who ultimately pleaded guilty to battery and was sentenced to eight years in prison. Caldemeyer wasn't having any of Swingley's protests. "You just offed this guy in cold blood," the judge told Swingley.

After his conviction, attorneys for Swingley appealed his conviction, arguing that "three gruesome and inflammatory autopsy slides" should not have been shown to jurors. The appeal was unsuccessful.

During comments to the jury in Swingley's murder trial, a prosecutor made an assertion that seemed particularly ominous in light of Muncie police investigators' belief that he had played a role in the Westside Park killings more than a decade before the Insco homicide: "James Swingley bragged three weeks before his indictment [for killing Insco] that you could get away with murder in Delaware County."

"ONE HOMICIDE AFTER ANOTHER"

Well before Kimberly Dowell and Ethan Dixon were killed in Westside Park in September 1985, their hometown of Muncie had what one veteran prosecutor recalled as a nearly overwhelming number of murders.

Richard Reed, Delaware County's chief deputy prosecutor at the time, remembered the period when he was working with Delaware County prosecutor Michael J. "Mick" Alexander as being particularly busy with homicides, most of which Alexander, Reed and the prosecutor's staff had to deal with. "I remember that in the first couple of years of his term, we just had one homicide after another," Reed said in a 2019 interview. "Just murder, murder, murder going on. We were inundated with homicides. We were trying them like crazy."

Strangely, one of the first homicide indictments to come out of Alexander's office was against a railroad company.

In February 1979, a month after Alexander took office, forty-two-year-old Eddy Anderson was killed and his wife injured when their car was struck by a train in the small southern Delaware County town of Oakville. Anderson's death was the second car-train fatality in rural Monroe Township in a week's time, but authorities believed there was culpability in the Anderson crash. Later in February 1979, a grand jury overseen by Alexander indicted Norfolk & Western Railway for reckless homicide. The grand jurors said the railroad company had set railway boxcars too close to the intersection, severely restricting the line of sight of motorists traveling through the crossing. In

March 1981, a jury found the railroad company morally responsible but not criminally liable in Anderson's death.

More traditional homicide investigations and cases followed during Alexander's term.

The body of Howard "Pete" Journay was found in the Mississinewa River, north of Muncie, in May 1979. The thirty-seven-year-old man had been beaten, and investigators believed he had been dead for weeks before he was found. Journay was described as a "rowdy" guy by veteran Delaware County police investigator Jerry Cook in a December 2012 "Cold Case Muncie" article in the *Star Press* newspaper that was written by the authors of this book. The article noted that no one had ever been arrested and charged in Journay's death.

In May 1980, Max and Margaret Williams were brutally killed in their home in the town of Yorktown, west of Muncie, during a burglary. The crime shocked and horrified Delaware County residents, some of whom said they didn't feel safe in their homes. Michael Webb was arrested, and although he was acquitted of killing Max Williams, he was convicted of stabbing Margaret Williams to death. In 1981, Webb was sentenced to forty years in prison. He was paroled in 2001 after serving half of his sentence, but he was returned to prison following parole violations, including theft and drunk driving. In 2007, Webb was found unconscious in his cell at the Pendleton Correctional Facility in Madison County. Webb later died, and coroners said no foul play was involved. The Webb case was the first investigated by a city–county homicide team, and his prosecution was spearheaded by Reed.

In May 1980, Delaware County authorities found themselves with four homicides in ten days. The murders of Max and Margaret Williams came first, on May 9. Russell Krull, who was seventy-three, was then found beaten to death in his Muncie home a few days later, and his killing was followed a few days after that by the death of Raymond Waldo, a resident of the small Delaware County town of Shideler. He was killed in his bed by a shotgun blast. David Wagner was arrested after police saw him driving Waldo's car. He was tried and convicted in Waldo's death. Lonnie Johnson was convicted of killing Krull, a retired grocer, and sentenced to sixty years in prison.

In early June 1980, within a month of the murders of Max and Margaret Williams, Russell Krull and Raymond Waldo, police found a Muncie man stabbed and mutilated in his Muncie apartment. The man's roommate, a woman whom he had met while they were being treated in a mental health facility, had stabbed him multiple times and cut off his penis.

In the same week, forty-year-old David Grimes was shot to death in his southside Muncie apartment. Earl Thomas Buley was arrested and ultimately convicted of reckless homicide.

Hulon Jewell, from Portland, Indiana, was killed by a shotgun blast in a westside Muncie house in December 1981. His daughter's boyfriend was initially charged with the crime, but the eighteen-year-old was later acquitted by a jury who decided that the younger man acted in self-defense.

Reed said that local police investigators were "stretched pretty thin" during those years after he and Alexander took office. "That had no effect on [the Westside] case though," Reed said, adding that even three and a half decades later, he was convinced that none of the investigators failed to follow up on viable leads.

SIXTEEN OF 160

By 1989, the murders of Ethan Dixon and Kimberly Dowell in Westside Park were four years old—and four years cold. Although Muncie police investigators returned to the boxes of reports and notes on the Dixon and Dowell killings many times over the years, authorities acknowledged before the end of the decade that the crime ranked high among other unsolved murders.

In a June 4, 1989 article in the *Muncie Star*, police said 160 murders had occurred in Delaware County since 1960 and that local police agencies had been able to resolve all but 16 of them. Muncie police captain Paul Cox, who had a role in the Westside Park investigation after the initial probe ran out of steam, said that in many of those unsolved cases, police had a strong suspect but were unable to make an arrest and seek charges. Cox said the increase in drug sales and use in Muncie resulted in an increase in homicides, as many of them grew out of drug crime.

Police cited the killing of Donald W. Phillips, a thirty-two-year-old eastside Muncie man whose body was found in a pickup truck along Butterfield Road. Cox said police had a suspect in Phillips's killing, "but [they didn't] have that one piece of evidence [they] need to crack the case."

The lack of physical evidence can sideline even investigations in which informants have named a murder suspect, Cox noted. "We've had cases where a dozen people come in and say that so-and-so did it. But we've not been able to get enough evidence to make an arrest."

The killings of Dixon and Dowell were also cited in the article. "As long as I have something to do with the detective division here, that case will remain open," Cox said. "We still, from time to time, pursue a lead in that case and worked one within the past few months that didn't turn up anything. But we keep all the paperwork, which fills about four boxes, in the office right next door here, so we can easily get to it and review it as the need arises."

The authors of this book returned to the Westside Park murders several times over the years, most notably with a 2010 article that recapped the crime and subsequent investigation. The story won several awards, including the 2011 Kent Cooper Award from the Indiana Associated Press, and kicked off a series, "Cold Case: Muncie," that eventually looked at more than two dozen unsolved murders in Muncie, Delaware County and the immediate area.

Some of the unsolved killings in "Cold Case: Muncie" were not included in the 1989 recounting, calling into question the accuracy of that "Sixteen of 160" number.

Notable by its omission from the 1989 story was the October 1962 slaying of Maggie Mae Fleming, who was shot through a window of her home as she held her young son. A November 2011 "Cold Case: Muncie" article recounted how Fleming's death had been forgotten by investigators but not, of course, by her grief-stricken children.

Also not cited in that 1989 article was the June 1974 slaying of William Gump, a well-known Muncie businessman who was shot and killed in his liquor store at the corner of Willard and Hackley Streets. Gump's murder was profiled in a November 2011 "Cold Case: Muncie" article. For that 2011 article, Muncie police acknowledged that they could no longer find a file on the Gump killing. It was a development that was all too common, unfortunately, in Muncie police investigations. The accidental—and otherwise—disposal and disruption of files for cases stretching back decades meant that investigators didn't even have old investigation paperwork to consult if they wanted to follow up on an unsolved homicide.

Those killings, and many others, had only a fraction of the notoriety of the Westside Park slayings. Fewer people remembered the crimes, and sometimes, few remembered the victims themselves.

THE TRAGIC DEATH OF SAM DRUMMER

He was, perhaps, Northside High School's most well-known alumnus, and he became the victim of an unsolved Muncie homicide.

Sam Drummer—one of the greatest high school basketball stars in a city that held that sport, above all others, in great reverence—attended Northside more than a decade before Ethan Dixon and Kimberly Dowell. And his shooting death came nearly that long, more than nine years, after the 1985 tragedy in Westside Park.

Drummer was not an Indiana native, as he was born in Mississippi in February 1956, but his family had moved to Muncie by the mid-1960s, when he was an elementary school student. (One of his friends growing up was Kimberly Dowell's older brother, Steve.)

From his earliest days at Northside High School, it was clear that Sam Drummer's skills on the basketball court made him something special. His senior season, in 1974 and 1975, saw the Titans go 24–3. Drummer averaged more than twenty-seven points per game that season and was named to the Indiana All-Star Team. Some of the top college basketball programs in the nation, including Bob Knight's Indiana Hoosiers, who were on the brink of an undefeated season and national championship, were interested in recruiting Drummer. However, he instead signed on to play for a NAIA school in North Carolina. He later ended up departing with the assistant coach who had recruited him before ever taking the court. Drummer ended up dividing his college career between two colleges in Georgia.

In 1979, he was drafted in the fifth round of the NBA draft by the Houston Rockets. However, he didn't make the team. Coaches and analysts—and

Drummer—later suggested he would have been far better prepared for an NBA career had his college career followed a more traditional route. Drummer then joined the Harlem Globetrotters, the barnstorming team that incorporated comedy and trick shots into a skilled brand of basketball.

In November 1980, Drummer and a teammate were arrested on cocaine charges in Brazil while traveling with the Globetrotters. He was deported, and his brief career as a professional basketball player was over. In the ensuing years, Drummer worked as a custodian at Ball State University, played in local recreation leagues and fathered five children.

In the early morning of February 4, 1995, authorities found a mortally wounded Drummer suffering from a gunshot wound in his upper left chest in a car that had crashed in the city's northeast Whitely neighborhood. Frantic resuscitation efforts were made as he was rushed by ambulance to Ball Memorial Hospital, but surgeons there quickly determined a .25-caliber bullet had pierced the basketball legend's heart, also striking his liver and right lung. At 2:05 a.m., Sam Drummer was pronounced dead.

Authorities have long believed Drummer was shot as he drove away from the Parkview Apartments Public Housing Complex. Word on the street was that he had failed to pay someone for crack cocaine.

There has been much talk over the past quarter century over who fired the fatal gunshot. There has not been enough information, however, to allow city police to make an arrest in the case. "That seems to happen a lot," city police sergeant Mike Engle told the authors of this book in a 2013 "Cold Case: Muncie" article on Drummer's death that was published in the *Star Press*. "They'll talk to each other, but they are not willing to put anything on paper or give a statement."

Robert Weller, deputy police chief at the time of Drummer's death, expressed frustration when talking to reporters a few weeks after the homicide. "We ran into a lot of people who talked to people who talked to somebody's brother," Weller said. "We have a lot of third- and fourth-hand information. I think there are people in the community who know exactly what happened that night. They're not the people coming forward."

Police, at times, hoped for breaks in the case when individuals who were rumored to be responsible in Drummer's death went to prison for other crimes. However, that didn't prompt anyone to come forward with new or more complete information.

For the 2013 "Cold Case" article, two of Drummer's daughters, Carol and Santana, spoke to the *Star Press*. They discussed the lack of closure for family members caused by the unsolved homicide. "I just feel like I would be at peace [should the case be solved]," said Santana, who was nine when her dad died.

Whatever substance abuse issues Sam Drummer battled at the end of his life—toxicology tests showed he was intoxicated and had cocaine in his system when he died—his daughters said he was a good father and never used drugs or appeared impaired in their presence. "Not at all," Santana said. "We couldn't tell at all."

For that 2013 article, a friend of Drummer said he had smoked crack cocaine with the basketball legend about an hour before his shooting. That man—who asked that his name not be used in the article—said he had urged Drummer to call it a night as they went their separate ways. It was advice that was apparently not taken. "When you are smoking cocaine [and] you are out of money, that is when the nightmare begins," he said, recalling the Parkview Apartments in the mid-1990s as "a no-man's land unless you were a veteran of the streets with a resume of criminal activity." His tragic end aside, the man said he would remember Sam Drummer as a "gentle giant [who] thrilled us all with his immense talent."

34

THE FOCUS NARROWS

Just shy of two years after the Westside Park killings, Muncie police, having already heard informants suggest that James "Jimmy" Swingley had some connection to the killings of Kimberly Dowell and Ethan Dixon, heard second- or third-hand information that Swingley had implicated himself in the crime.

Swingley had, just two months earlier, failed crucial questions in a PSE, or a lie detector test, administered by Muncie police. Swingley failed because the PSE indicated he was "showing deception" on three questions about the slayings in Westside Park, including, "Do you know who killed the young people in the park?" and "Did you kill the young people in the park?" Muncie police detective Nathan Sloan said in a 2019 interview, "He failed all the pertinent questions about Westside Park."

In November 1987, an informant developed by a Muncie police investigator recounted how Swingley had gone to the Muncie home of Albert Hirst the night of the killings. Hirst and Swingley knew each other, police said, and on that night, Swingley went to Hirst and told him that he had killed two people. Hirst didn't believe him, at which point, the informant said, Swingley pulled out a .38-caliber handgun and held it to Hirst's head. "I've already killed two people tonight, and I'll blow your brains out," Swingley reportedly told Hirst. It was a threat that Hirst recounted to others, who, in turn, told police.

In March 2012, Muncie police detective Nathan Sloan, who had been newly assigned to review the Westside case, contacted two women close to Hirst. Each told the investigator that they didn't know Swingley and had never heard about anyone putting a gun to Hirst's head. Albert Hirst died in November 2006, long before Sloan was assigned to the case, so he could contact him to confirm or discount the story. And several years after, Swingley was in prison for killing Brian Insco.

Sloan's years-long review of the Westside Park killings often followed paths that promised answers but led to dead ends. Nevertheless, even as Sloan was able to flesh out some leads and discount some theories, the detective's focus narrowed further on Jimmy Swingley. Interviews conducted by Sloan continued to link Swingley and his associates to a Chevrolet Monte Carlo, a car that some witnesses saw in the park the night of the killings.

In March 2012, a person close to Swingley who was interviewed by police, said a Swingley associate had owned a Monte Carlo. The man told police that, early in the morning after the murders, Swingley woke him up and said that a man who he had been with had shot two people in Westside Park after an argument. Swingley didn't specify that he was in the park, but the man believed that he was. The man also told police that the Monte Carlo had been driven to Arizona and "crushed." A woman interviewed by police at around the same time in 2012 confirmed that the Swingley associate had driven a Monte Carlo.

In 2012, investigators reviewed a report from a law enforcement agency outside the Muncie Police Department that had been told that the Westside Park killings resulted from a dispute in the park. The report said that Ethan Dixon had pulled a knife to defend himself and that he was shot by someone in a group that included Swingley. The suspects fled the park in a dark Chrysler Cordoba, a car that shared many visual characteristics with the Chevrolet Monte Carlo.

Two years later, another woman who had been close to Swingley told Sloan that Swingley had driven a 1978 or 1979 Monte Carlo.

In April 2012, Sloan and another detective traveled to the state prison in Michigan City, Indiana, to speak to Swingley. Swingley became hostile when he saw the investigators. "Fuck you," Swingley said. "I don't care what you want. Fuck off." The detectives left the prison. It would be several years before Sloan had another face-to-face encounter with Jimmy Swingley.

"YOU TALKING ABOUT THE PARK? KIDS?"

In August 2013, Muncie police detective Nathan Sloan met with a correctional officer who worked at the Delaware County Jail. Sloan wanted to meet with the woman because she was on James "Jimmy" Swingley's list of approved visitors in prison. The woman, whom we'll call Edith Evans here, met with Sloan and a county police investigator in an interview room at the Delaware County Sheriff's Office.

Sloan asked Evans about several people whose names had been cited as having some kind of connection to local crime and murder cases. Evans had some knowledge of several people in cases unrelated to the killings of Ethan Dixon and Kimberly Dowell. Then, Sloan asked Evans about her connection to Swingley, and she answered that they were cousins. Swingley was in prison for the murder of Brian Insco at the time.

Sloan asked if Evans knew of any other crimes her cousin had committed. "You talking about the park? Kids?" Evans answered. Evans said a family member had told her that Swingley had stolen his gun and shot and killed the two teenagers in Westside Park. The family member who linked Swingley to the killings of Dowell and Dixon was deceased, Evans said, although she cited other family members who might know something. And she said she never knew the relative who implicated Swingley to be a liar.

Evans also told Sloan that Swingley had killed someone behind a southside Muncie tavern, although records don't seem to indicate any homicide associated with that tavern. Evans also confirmed to Sloan a previous account that said Swingley's brother, Jackie, had died in a physical altercation with Swingley, not Jackie's wife.

Person after person who knew Swingley told Sloan that they had heard he was connected to the Westside Park killings—or that they believed that either he had committed the murders or was capable of it. This included Swingley's mother. Desiree Dawn spoke to Sloan at her Muncie home in February 2014. She told Sloan that she had heard rumors that her son had been arrested in connection with the Westside Park killings and that she thought he had been capable of killing Dixon and Dowell. Swingley's mother, who said she had put the boy up for adoption, also placed her son in the room when his brother Jackie was killed in January 1981.

In September 2018, Sloan and a county police investigator spoke to a man in the town of Eaton, outside Muncie. Sloan told the man—called Mark Mason here (a pseudonym)—that he wanted to ask him about the Westside Park slayings in 1985. "Oh, fucking Jimmy Swingley," Mason replied. Mason went on to tell the investigators what he said he had been told by Swingley not long after the killings. Mason said Swingley had been in Westside Park that night to sell cocaine. Swingley and Dixon got into an argument, and Swingley took a gun and shot Dixon. Sloan asked Mason about Kimberly Dowell and received a chilling reply. Mason said Swingley was trying to shoot Ethan Dixon but missed "and hit that fucking bitch."

Mason picked Swingley out of a photo lineup and also detailed for the detectives what he knew about Swingley's role in the death of his brother, Jackie Swingley.

"MY SON WAS A SWEET BOY"

few days after Nancy Vogelgesang died, on Christmas Eve in 1987, authorities performed tests to determine if Kimberly Dixon's mother had also been the victim of foul play. Just after her funeral, five days after her death, Nancy's body was quietly removed from Meeks Mortuary, and an autopsy was performed. Two years and three months after Kimberly's death, police wanted to see if her mother had been poisoned.

The autopsy showed no sign of foul play, and Kimberly's stepfather, Don Vogelgesang, cited his past cooperation with investigators, specifically in consenting to the examination, in an interview with Muncie police detective Nathan Sloan about twenty-eight years later.

In April 2013, Sloan returned two guns to Vogelgesang that police had seized years earlier. The guns had no connection to the killings, police said. While he was talking to Sloan in 2013, Vogelgesang recounted how the evening of September 28, 1985, had occurred, including the concerns of Nancy, Kimberly's mother, when the girl hadn't come home by 11:00 p.m. Vogelgesang, driving Nancy's Olds Cutlass, circled the McDonald's on Tillotson Avenue, looking for the kids, and then, he drove up to Westside Park, where Nancy believed the two might have taken a pizza. Vogelgesang said a police officer stopped him at the park's entrance. He told the officer that his daughter might be in the park. Vogelgesang tried to call Nancy. She didn't answer, but she arrived at the park shortly after. At some point, the Vogelgesangs were told that Kimberly had indeed been killed in the park.

BECKETT BRONZE CO., INC.

401 WEST 23rd STREET
P.O. BOX 2425
MUNCIE, INDIANA 47307-0425

PHONE: (765) 282-2261
FAX: (765) 282-2268
www.beckettbronze.com

April 19, 2002

Capt. Robert Weller
Muncie Police Department
City Hall
300 N. High St.
Muncie, IN 47305

Dear Capt. Weller,

Kay and I wanted to thank you for taking the time to advise us about the efforts you have been making on investigating our son's murder. Although there isn't too much new on the case, we believe that you and your team will continue to do whatever is possible to resolve it.

As I mentioned before, we would be willing to finance testing or other expenses which you might deem worthwhile in the event that funds were not available from the city. If anything new were to show up on our end we will certainly be in contact.

My son was a sweet boy. He was bright and affectionate. His friends have turned out well. Ethan and Kimberly would have been assets to society had they lived. Maybe one day they will have justice. Kay and I believe that is also your hope.

Thanks again for taking your time and the time of your officers to meet with us.

Very truly yours,

Steve Dixon

Vice-President

MANUFACTURERS OF BRONZE BUSHINGS–BEARINGS–CONTINUOUS CAST BARS–SINCE 1913

Steve Dixon, Ethan's father, wrote this letter to Muncie Police Department officials in April 2002. *Courtesy of Muncie Police Department.*

On October 4, Vogelgesang went to the Muncie Police Department offices at Muncie's city hall. This was when he was interviewed and given a "lie detector" test. In the 2013 interview, Sloan asked Vogelgesang if he had told police, as investigators in 1985 recounted in a confidential case report, something like, "If I did this, you're going to have to tell me I did it." Vogelgesang remembered making the statement and attributed it to tiredness at the time and that he didn't mean anything by it. Vogelgesang told Sloan that he had consented to Nancy's autopsy even though he was still angry at police.

Sloan said, after his interview with Vogelgesang, that he didn't believe the stepfather was, "in any way," a legitimate suspect.

When contacted in 2019 by the authors of this book, Vogelgesang referred to the toll that the suspicion of his involvement in the killings had taken on his life over the decades.

Steve Dixon, Ethan's father, declined to be interviewed for this book when he was contacted in 2019. Even in two brief telephone conversations, the older Dixon's anguish, thirty-four years after the death of his son, was palpable.

In speaking to Sloan in June 2013, Steve Dixon was emotional in talking about his son's murder. He said that, at some point before the murders, the Dixons had taken a switchblade from Ethan, who had apparently acquired the knife after he had been bullied. It was unknown if the knife had ended up in Ethan's possession again or even if it was the same knife that was found on the dashboard of the young man's Volkswagen Rabbit the night he and Kimberly were killed. The older Dixon couldn't identify the knife when shown a photograph. Steve Dixon said he was fairly certain that his son did not own a gun, ruling out an explanation that the holster found in Ethan's car was his. Ethan's car had been sold, through a third party, to an unknown individual, his father said.

Dixon wrote a heartfelt letter to Muncie police in 2002, thanking the detectives for their diligence over the years in pursuing an arrest in the case and some closure for the families. "Although there isn't too much new on the case, we believe that you and your team will continue to do whatever is possible to resolve it," Dixon wrote. "My son was a sweet boy. He was bright and affectionate. His friends have turned out well. Ethan and Kimberly would have been assets to society had they lived. Maybe one day, they will have justice." The letter, framed, hung in the police offices at Muncie City Hall for many years.

The lone exception to the reluctance of the families to talk on the record over the years about the killings of Ethan and Kimberly has been Anthony Dowell, Kimberly's father and a longtime physician.

37

"IT'S A DOWELL. THERE'S NO QUESTION."

Physician Anthony Dowell has spent much of his life in Muncie, but he was born in the small town of Du Quoin, Illinois, about ninety miles southeast of St. Louis, in March 1938.

Anthony's father, Omar, who was from Chicago, was a longtime regional manager for A.B. Dick Co., a manufacturer of office supplies. (As a student at Northwestern University, Omar Dowell had a future celebrity as a roommate for a semester: Johnny Weissmuller, who would go on to win five gold medals as an Olympic swimmer and then play Tarzan in a series of movies in the 1930s and 1940s.) In 1944, Omar, who was, by then, living with his wife, Mildred, and six-year-old son, Anthony "Tony," in Huntington, West Virginia, arranged to open an A.B. Dick franchise in Muncie, and the family became Hoosiers.

When Tony was a student at McKinley Junior High School, a cheerleader named Nancy Mitchell first caught his eye. They became better acquainted as students at Muncie Central High School. "Good lady," Dowell recalled more than six decades later. "National Honor Society. Very popular girl, very reasonable. A level-headed girl. Very well respected." When they were Central seniors, Dowell made a couple of attempts to ask Nancy out. He was not successful.

After graduation, in 1955, Tony Dowell attended Wabash College in Crawfordsville. Later, as a college sophomore, he was back in Muncie for a visit at the Tally Ho restaurant on the Ball State Teachers College campus, when he ran into Nancy Mitchell, who was attending Ball State. A friend encouraged Dowell to ask Nancy—who was at the Tally Ho with her sorority sisters—out again, despite his failed attempts to do so in high school. "I tried again, and this time, I was successful," he recalled.

The couple was later married in the chapel of High Street Methodist Church in July 1958. Their first child, their son Stephen, was born the following year, while his father was a freshman medical student at the Indiana University School of Medicine in Indianapolis.

The young family lived in Indianapolis until 1963, when Tony Dowell graduated from medical school. Nancy, during those years, worked as an elementary school teacher for Indianapolis Public Schools. "She was a wonderful teacher," Tony Dowell recalled. "She taught second, third and fourth grade."

Dowell then accepted an academic internship at Duke University, prompting the family's move to Durham, North Carolina, where Nancy also taught in the local school system. "I did my internship, my residency and my fellowship, in pulmonary disease," he said.

After a two-year stint in the U.S. Air Force as a medical officer, which Tony spent mainly at Wright-Patterson Air Force Base near Dayton, Ohio, Dowell returned to Duke University—this time, as a faculty member. "I had

A young Kimberly Dowell. *Courtesy of Anthony Dowell.*

my own research laboratory," he said. "I was working on environmental effects on lungs."

It was in Durham, in October 1969, that Nancy delivered the couple's second child, a daughter, Kimberly. A half-century later, her father still vividly recalled the first time he saw Kim. "She was in Nancy's arms," he said. "I took one look at Kim and said, 'It's a Dowell. There's no question.' She looked like my father's grandmother—looked like my dad in a lot of ways."

In 1971, veteran Muncie physician Maurice Schulhof came to Durham with an offer for Tony Dowell. "He said, 'Tony, we have a wonderful opportunity in Muncie, your hometown, to do real medicine and make a real impact,'" Dowell said of the proposal that he join the staff at the Muncie Clinic on West Washington Street. Dowell said he and his wife made the decision to "come back here" at that time. "I felt the pull back to my roots," he said. "My hometown."

The Dowells eventually moved into a home they had built along Forest Avenue. Steve, and later Kim, entered the city school system. After about five years of living in Muncie, however, Tony and Nancy Dowell's marriage fell apart. "It was a confusing point in my life," Tony recalled more than forty years later. In addition to maintaining his private medical practice, Dowell was the director for the Muncie Center for Medical Education, a leader in the American Lung Association and a teacher. "I basically was working probably sixteen hours a day," he said. "I had more on my plate than I probably should have....I left Nancy all of our savings, the house [and] moved into an apartment."

The Dowells, from that point forward, were a two-household family. Both Tony and Nancy eventually found other spouses. Kim, while she lived with her mother, remained a vital part of father's life. As she moved into her high school years, planning her future became a large part of their relationship. "Kim would come down a lot and spent time with me," he recalled. "We would take her to different cities to look at colleges. We went to Gettysburg, we went to Earlham, we went to I.U., Purdue, all over. I think that her preference was Purdue. But she liked Earlham, too." (According to correspondence between her parents in the wake of her death, Kim also hoped to spend a year studying in France.)

Tony Dowell recalled a day he took Kim to Standt's Fine Jewelry in downtown Muncie to buy her a watch. Some longtime friends were in the shop, and they noted the pride Tony Dowell had in his daughter. "I said, 'Oh, yeah, she's just a great, great kid,'" he said. "I remember that day."

38

"WE WERE ALL SUSPECTS"

Tony Dowell was "sound asleep" in his Indianapolis home in the early morning hours of September 29, 1985, when the phone rang. It was his son, Steve, calling from Dallas, Texas, where the younger Dowell then lived. "He said, 'Dad, I've got bad news,'" Tony Dowell recalled during a 2019 interview. "He said, 'Dad, Kim's been shot.'" Dowell said that his first response to that stunning news was to ask Steve, "How bad is it?" He remembered his son responded, "Dad, she's a goner."

Tony Dowell and his second wife, Sharon, had moved a few months earlier to Indianapolis, where he had accepted a job as a clinical research scientist at Eli Lilly and Company. After the move, Kim had spent several weekends with her father and stepmother at their new home. "She was a successful kid," her father said. "She didn't get in trouble. She was disciplined. She was courteous. She used good grammar. Teachers liked her....She had great friends. The kids that she ran around with were all from wonderful families."

Earlier that year, before the move to Indianapolis, Kim had brought her new boyfriend, Ethan Dixon, to meet her father at Tony Dowell's Muncie home. "I remember when he left our house, I told Sharon, '[Kim] likes him, and they seem to get along well together, so I have no objection.' I couldn't put my finger on any reason they shouldn't be dating....He was a good student. He was president of his junior class. He came from a nice family."

Dowell recalls a later conversation he had with his daughter in the back yard of his Muncie home, when she was apparently thinking about her future. "She asked me one time, we were sitting in the back yard, she said,

'Dad, what do you think about living together?' I said, 'Well, it's complicated, Kim. Sometimes, people live together for a while and then they marry, and they have a good relationship. Sometimes, it doesn't work out.'"

Tony Dowell's last conversation with his daughter was over the phone on the morning of the day she died.

> *I called her up and said, "Are you coming over?" She had spent the previous weekend with Sharon and me in* [Indianapolis]. *We had a great time. She loved Broad Ripple and Glendale* [Mall]. *I called Kim that morning and said, "You're coming over?" Because I had some things planned for us to do. And she said no. She sounded not normal. Something was going on. I said, "What's wrong? Are you sick?" She said no—didn't want to talk much. I knew something was going on.*

More than thirty-four years later, Dowell still doesn't know what seemed to be troubling his daughter that morning—or if it was somehow related to the tragedy that unfolded that night.

That evening, Dowell and his wife had dinner with friends. The names of those friends were later provided to police, as virtually everyone connected to Kim and Ethan Dixon were asked to verify where they were at the time of the slayings. "We were all suspects," Tony Dowell recalled.

After learning of his daughter's death from his son, Steve, Dowell decided to go to Muncie "almost immediately." He said, "I drove over that morning, and it was just beginning to get sunlight when I drove [into Muncie]. I drove over to Westside Park, with all the yellow tape."

At the park's entrance, Tony saw Jack Maddy, a city police officer he had known for years. "I'd been his mom's doctor," Dowell recalled. "He had the worst look on his face. He said, 'Tony, I can't let you in the park.' I said, 'I understand.' He was just crestfallen."

Shortly before Kim's calling hours at Meeks Mortuary, Tony Dowell recalled a brief problem that was quickly corrected, when her mother noted her dress "had been placed on backwards."

"She had a gunshot wound in her left temple," he said. "I think they were able to cover that with her hair. I think they did a great job. Me, I'm not an open casket kind of guy. But with a kid and this kind of publicity and all that was going on, I think it was a good idea. And Ethan's was open casket, too. So, I think it was probably a good decision."

Dowell attended Ethan's funeral at St. Mary's Catholic Church, and of course, he was at Kim's service at High Street United Methodist Church. He

Kimberly Dowell. *Courtesy of Anthony Dowell.*

still recalls stepping out into the sanctuary and walking past Kim's coffin. He remembers being surprised and moved by the large number of mourners on hand. "The place was packed," he said. "It was a very nice service."

At that time, Dowell remembered, his focus was not really on the perpetrator who had taken his daughter's life. "I was trying to get myself and the family through a tough situation," he said. But after the funeral, as he stepped outside the church, where the hearse was waiting, he recalled looking at the throngs of people assembled outside and "wondering if the perpetrators were in the crowd."

The police officers investigating the Westside slayings—later including some high school classmates of Dowell—provided him with updates at times, such as they were. "They just did not have a clue," he said.

He recalled one meeting at the police chief's office that did not include Kim's mother or stepfather "because Don was being publicized as being a suspect." Dowell said he had no information that caused him to believe Don Vogelgesang had committed the slayings. Kim never reported any problems whatsoever with her stepfather, he said, and his former wife assured him "that's nothing we need to be concerned about."

Dowell was taken aback when he heard investigators had, at one point, hired a psychic. "I thought, 'What a waste of taxpayers' money,'" he said. "They must have been desperate. My heart goes out to them, the pressure they were under....It was a tough situation."

Kimberly Dowell was laid to rest in Muncie's Elm Ridge Cemetery, next to her paternal grandfather, Omar, who had died a year before she was born. Omar's wife, Mildred, outlived him by a dozen years, and near the end of her life, she told their son she preferred to be laid to rest with her family members in Illinois. That left the space by her husband open when Kim died four years later. "I remember a couple of times I came back over from Indianapolis and just spent a little time there at the grave site," Tony Dowell said. "And I thought, 'She's not really here.' And I feel that way about my mom, my dad. There are other people who feel differently [about grave visitation], and that's fine. It's just a matter of faith."

Dowell, who moved back to Muncie more than thirty years ago and now lives with his third wife, Betsy, doesn't know whether the slayings of his daughter and Ethan Dixon will ever be solved. "Nothing surprises me," he said. "Whoever was involved, if it was a mind-blowing illumination, it wouldn't surprise me one damn bit. It was a human being. And it was an evil act. We all see evil in this world."

Would an arrest—or at least a determination of who was responsible—bring closure? "Not really for me," Dowell said. "If Kim were here, she'd say, 'Dad, don't obsess about this. Go on with your life.' That's the kind of person she was."

A lifelong Methodist, Dowell credits his religious beliefs and his medical background with helping him survive the loss of his daughter. "I have a perspective of life, probably because of my upbringing, my religious background, my medical training," he said. "It is what it is, and don't draw conclusions that you shouldn't be drawing. Let things play out and accept them for what they are. My feeling about Kim is I just feel honored to have had the sixteen years with her, and [I] look back on the good times rather than dwell on what could have been—should have been. I think it's a healthier way. That just works for me."

39

THE PROSECUTORS

During what turned into decades of frustrated investigations into the Westside Park killings, few elected officials watched developments in the case as closely as the men who served as the Delaware County prosecutor. "We were itching for them to bring us a case," Richard Reed said in a 2019 interview. "We wanted them to solve that case."

Reed was the county's chief deputy prosecutor when Kimberly Dixon and Ethan Dowell were killed in September 1985. Reed's longtime friend and law partner Michael J. "Mick" Alexander was Delaware County's prosecuting attorney. Alexander had been elected in 1978, taking office in January 1979 and holding the post until the end of 1986.

Alexander was known for his aggressive courtroom questioning of witnesses and combative stance in local Democratic Party politics. After leaving office as prosecutor, he became a defense attorney, often defending people charged with murder and other serious crimes. A third-degree black belt in karate, Alexander could back up his words with action if necessary. Alexander died in 2017 at the age of seventy. In his obituary, his family noted, "The doctors and nurses were grateful the family was there to calm him and translate his very colorful verbiage."

After Alexander's death, then-prosecutor Jeffrey Arnold noted that Alexander was "the ultimate adversary" on the opposite side of the courtroom. What Alexander could have done to a suspect in the Westside Park case can only be imagined.

Although Alexander made his mark on the prosecutor's office for eight years, no prosecutor had more time in office in recent decades than Reed. Reed, like Alexander, was a Democrat, and he was elected in 1990, taking office in January 1991, when the Westside Park crime was a little more than five years old. He recalled asking police detectives, including Muncie Police Department investigator Steve Stanley, for updates on the case. "Although they never brought us a case, we'd be talking about some other case, and I'd ask about the park," Reed said. "They never gave up on the case. Steve Stanley never gave up on the case."

Reed's four terms made him the longest-serving county prosecutor in recent local history. He announced in early 2005 that he would not seek reelection in 2006 and that he was planning to retire in January 2007.

40

THE HOMICIDE TEAM

Thanks to what one veteran lawman called "childish stuff," the city of Muncie and Delaware County's joint homicide team, which was composed of police officers and specialists in their fields, was not in existence in September 1985, when Kimberly Dowell and Ethan Dixon were killed in Westside Park. The team had been created and disbanded within a less than two-year period, and it was only reformed after the Muncie Police Department's Westside Park investigation had grown cold.

On January 7, 1980, Delaware County sheriff Gary Camichael and Muncie police chief Gene Hayden—the former an elected Republican and the latter appointed by Republican mayor Alan Wilson—announced the formation of a team that would "investigate all homicides in Muncie and Delaware County." The two said a "team" approach to investigating homicides was long needed and cited "problems" with communications between investigators and issues with trial preparation.

Twenty-three-year veteran cop Jack Stonebraker Jr., a Muncie police lieutenant, was to oversee the homicide team. Stonebraker later served as a prosecutor's office investigator, and he was elected as Delaware County's coroner. In the previous year, Stonebraker had been assigned as city police liaison to the office of County Prosecutor Michael J. "Mick" Alexander. Stonebraker, with his white hair and beard and deep, authoritative voice, was an imposing figure who, nevertheless, was known for playing Santa Claus each Christmas at office gatherings and at the Delaware County Children's Home.

Veteran Muncie police investigators and officials Marvin Campbell (*left*) and Don Scroggins (*right*). *Author's collection.*

It was Stonebraker who came up with the idea of a homicide team, Carmichael and Hayden told *Muncie Evening Press* reporter Joe Canan. Canan reported that "incomplete or unclear" reports turned in to the prosecutor's office were one reason behind the creation of the team. Breakdowns in communication among investigators were also cited.

The team also included Indiana State Police and Ball State University investigators and officers from smaller town jurisdictions when needed.

On the team, veteran detectives, like county police investigator Jerry Cook and city police officer Don Scroggins, would fulfill tasks that included photographing crime scenes and interrogating suspects, respectively, while longtime officers would fill other roles. City police investigator George Wilson did double duty as a lie detector examiner and hypnosis expert.

It wasn't common but it wasn't unheard of in the late 1970s and early 1980s for Muncie police officers to use hypnosis in efforts to solve crimes. In December 1981, the *Muncie Star* reported on the use of the technique to help resolve a pair of robberies, one in Muncie and one in Indianapolis, that had resulted in a would-be robber being shot and killed. Muncie police used hypnosis on a witness to the Muncie crime to come up with a composite drawing of the robber that was matched to the robber in the morgue in Indianapolis. Nevertheless, some were skeptical. Richard Reed, Delaware County's chief deputy prosecutor, said he hoped he would never have to try a case against a defendant in which hypnosis had been used. "I'm sure the defense would have a field day with that," Reed told the newspaper.

Within two years of the creation of the city–county team, fifteen investigators would come together to respond when a homicide was committed in any corner of Delaware County. Each member had a specialty, like shooting video of crime scenes, and after an initial investigation was complete, team members would meet and decide if more investigation was needed. In September 1981, for example, the homicide team spent four days in the home of slaying victim Marie Isenhart. In a one-month period, the team investigated five homicides.

Was the team effective? In November 1981, the *Muncie Star* reported that all homicides investigated by the city–county team had resulted in convictions. But a month earlier, the Muncie Police Department, under Hayden, had withdrawn from the city–county team and formed its own homicide team with little or no notice to the official joint team. Hayden said some of the city officers suffered from "bruised egos" because they were not included in the city–county homicide team. "I'm not saying we can do it any better, but morale-wise, it will be much better," Hayden said. A "morale problem" plagued city police officers who were not part of the city–county homicide team, Hayden said.

The new city team was composed of nineteen Muncie Police Department officers. Prosecutor Alexander told the newspaper he was "skeptical" of the new city team, and Sheriff Carmichael said he doubted the "morale problem" story. "It is more childish stuff," Carmichael said. Alexander said the creation of the city team was typical of the city administration's "usual way of cooperation." The prosecutor said, "There'll be different people running around doing different things, and the paperwork will be in a hodgepodge fashion." He added that he didn't fault the effectiveness of the individual city police investigators but the likely administration of the team.

Delaware Superior Court 1 judge Robert Barnet Jr., who had served as a deputy prosecutor in the 1970s, told the newspaper that he thought the city–county team had been professional and added that he wished such a team had been in existence when he was prosecuting cases. Veteran defense attorney J.A. Cummins, the brother-in-law of Prosecutor Alexander, said the city–county team had been effective. "One of the best tools of

Jack Stonebraker, a longtime Muncie police investigator who played a pivotal role in local homicide investigations. *Author's collection.*

a defense attorney is lack of cooperation among police departments," Cummins said.

In an opinion column on October 29, 1981, *Muncie Evening Press* columnist Dick Stodghill was sarcastic about the reasons behind the city's new team. "Sounds like we're going to have to start killing each other off a little faster to keep everybody busy," Stodghill wrote. "The combined city–county–state homicide unit was batting a thousand this year," Stodgill added. "Following that act, it sure would be embarrassing to strike out." Stodghill cited phrases like "our own crimes" from a letter to the editor from a police official and said the move sounded like possessiveness and had a "provincial ring" to it.

By December 1986, in the wake of elections that turned over the administration of both the City of Muncie and offices like prosecutor and coroner, officials announced that, come January 1, 1987, the city–county homicide team would be reestablished under the supervision of incoming Delaware County coroner Jack Stonebraker, Muncie police chief Don Scroggins, sheriff-elect Dan Elliott and incoming prosecutor Ray Brassart. The new team would include not only city and county investigators but also officers from local towns, Ball State University and, this time, the Muncie Fire Department.

The reinstatement of the homicide team would come about fifteen months after the Westside Park killings. There's no indication that the new team ever worked on the case, which, by that time, had moved out of the headlines and, presumably, off of the desks of investigators.

41
SECOND-GUESSING THE INVESTIGATORS

With a high-profile murder investigation, it's fairly common that experienced investigators second guess the conclusions reached by the detectives working the case.

With a double-homicide case, like the Westside Park investigation, longtime police professionals with Muncie backgrounds have strong opinions about how the case was handled. But perhaps because Muncie is a small city and the circles police travel in are small—and because of the sensitivity of the slayings of two teenagers going unsolved for decades—veteran investigators are fairly circumspect in how they talk publicly about the case.

"Not being able to read the case report, I'm not sure who was interviewed, who gave statements....Everybody should have given statements, including the person who found the victims," Richard Heath, a longtime Muncie cop, detective and police chief, said in a 2019 interview.

Heath, at the age of eighty-five, talked about his background in Muncie law enforcement and his slight involvement in the Westside case. A Muncie native, Korean War veteran and twenty-year military reserve officer, Heath was chief of police under Mayor Robert Cunningham and left the department in 1984, a year before Ethan Dixon and Kimberly Dowell were killed.

After leaving Muncie, Heath worked on a white-collar crime task force and was on the staff of the district attorney's office in Milwaukee, Wisconsin, in 1991, when serial killer and cannibal Jeffrey Dahmer's crimes were uncovered. Heath sat in on and recorded twenty hours of

Richard Heath, a veteran Muncie police officer who was asked to look into the Westside Park case after he left the force in Muncie. *Author's collection.*

interviews with Dahmer, who was killed in prison by another inmate in 1994.

Heath was asked to return to Muncie after the Westside Park killings—but not by Muncie police investigators. He was asked to check on the investigation by Muncie attorney Charles "Chic" Clark, who represented Don Vogelgesang, Kimberly Dowell's stepfather. Marvin Campbell, the deputy chief of police at the time, had focused on Vogelgesang as the likely suspect. "Chic Clark and I went to school together," Heath recalled. "He told me they were blaming the stepfather and said, 'I'd like you to look into this.' I came down and talked to the chief and said, 'I'd like to talk to somebody in the detective bureau.'" He was able to have those conversations, but Muncie police declined to let him look at the Westside Park case file.

Heath found that, even among Muncie detectives, there was still some doubt as to who committed the crime. While Campbell had always focused on Vogelgesang, others in the department thought they knew who the killer was, Heath said. Heath said it was "awfully hard" to judge the Muncie police department's investigation without full access to the files.

Jerry Cook was a lifelong cop and investigator before retiring. By the time of the killings, he had been in the Delaware County Sheriff's Department for more than eight years. Since the sheriff's office has countywide jurisdiction, county investigators like Cook could have looked into the Westside Park case, but there was no agreement to do so since a city–county homicide team was not active at the time. So, county police investigators steered clear of the case. "We were hearing rumors about the stepdad," Cook recalled in a 2019 interview. "I don't remember specifically what they were. It's been too long ago." About the killings of Dowell and Dixon, Cook said, "I have no theory. I never had the information. Never saw the case [file]."

Cook said he does regret that the city–county homicide team wasn't formed at the time and couldn't look into the case. "We had people who were good at talking to people, good at talking to witnesses, good at photographs and fingerprints and crime scenes. It worked out really well." Cook said he would have put those officers with experience in specialized investigations to work if the city–county squad had been active.

Cook said police officials in the early 1980s wanted the two departments—city and county—to work separately. "They had some strange ideas about how things should be done."

42

THE APPEAL

Not long after he was sentenced to prison for killing Brian Insco, James "Jimmy" Swingley began trying to win his freedom.

On April 8, 1999, Delaware Circuit Court judge Steven Caldemeyer sentenced Swingley to sixty-five years, the maximum sentence. Very quickly, the attorneys for Swingley tried to appeal his conviction on the grounds that the judge allowed jurors in the trial to see photographic slides that were prejudicial to his case. Three of the slides were "gruesome and inflammatory" autopsy slides that showed the severity of the wound to Insco's neck. It was an injury that all but severed the man's head from his body. But an appeal based on that tactic didn't work, and he remained in the Wabash Valley Correctional Facility, an Indiana Department of Correction prison, in Carlisle, Indiana.

Swingley, as many prison inmates do, participated in programs designed to educate and rehabilitate prisoners—programs frequently cited by inmates in efforts to win sentence modifications, relocations to other facilities or early release. His court file, which is several inches thick, contains a certificate that says he completed the Department of Correction Mental Health Services Anger Management Psycho-Educational Self-Study Program on December 29, 2000. In April 2001, another certificate noted, Swingley completed the Christian Doctrine Volume One course of the American Bible Academy.

In asking that his sentence be modified or suspended outright, Swingley noted that his daughter was the manager of a fast-food restaurant in Louisville, Kentucky, and had promised he would be hired to work there if he were to be released. He also said he would live with his daughter in Louisville.

Another daughter wrote a letter saying that Swingley, although he had been locked up since she was fourteen, always wrote letters to her children on their birthdays. "They think he is the neatest thing since sliced bread.... He is so very much loved and missed by me and our family." A third daughter noted that Swingley had twelve grandchildren he could have been spending time with. In 2015, a ten-year-old grandchild wrote a letter seeking sentence modification for Swingley, noting that he had only seen him during jail visits.

In a letter to Delaware Circuit Court judge Marianne Vorhees, Caldemeyer's successor on the bench, Swingley himself wrote, "I have been locked up over ten years on this commitment." He said he "was on the drugs and alcohol real bad" at the time of Brian Insco's murder. At the age of forty-six, Swingley wrote to the judge, "I have grown up since my arrest, grown up in here. I now have my priorities in order. I now realize what is most important in my life, and it is my family, my grandchildren, my daughters, my fiancé, my mom. I'm a completely different person than the one who walked through those prison gates so many years ago."

Judge Vorhees, in March 2015, denied Swingley's petition for a sentence modification, and in April 2016, she denied his petition for more good behavior time to be credited to his sentence.

Included in the court record of his unsuccessful appeals was a long list of conduct violations that Indiana Department of Correction authorities said he committed while in prison, including threatening, vulgarity, unauthorized possession of property, tattooing or self-mutilation, battery without a weapon and other offenses.

43

THE SECOND ENCOUNTER

More than six years after their first encounter in an Indiana prison interview room, Muncie police detective Nathan Sloan and convicted killer James "Jimmy" Swingley met again.

The first time, in April 2012, Swingley had been angry and dismissive in his reaction to seeing Sloan and another detective waiting to talk to him. "Fuck you," Swingley had told Sloan. "I don't care what you want. Fuck off." The interview ended before it began. But in late 2018, Sloan went to the Wabash Valley Correctional Facility, where Swingley was serving time for killing Brian Insco, armed with a body warrant to get a sample of Swingley's DNA.

Sloan had prepared for weeks for his second chance to interview Swingley. With help from someone with legal expertise, Sloan prepared a court document detailing what was, in effect, his case against Swingley. The goal: to persuade a judge to issue a warrant ordering Swingley to submit a DNA sample. The sample could be compared to any DNA possibly collected from the scene of Kimberly Dowell and Ethan Dixon's killings—in particular, from the leather gun holster found in Ethan's car.

In the request for a body warrant, Sloan detailed evidence that searching six years of interviews and records had turned up:

- Swingley's girlfriend at the time of the September 1985 slayings lived just 1,300 feet away from where the bodies of Dixon and Dowell were found.

- Swingley had reportedly told an acquaintance in January 1986 that he was afraid he would be contacted by police about the killings.

- On August 17, 1986, Swingley gave his name as Kevin L. Dixon when he was pulled over by a Muncie police officer for running a stop sign.

- Swingley, on January 7, 1987, had told an associate that he had been in Westside Park the night of the killings to collect a debt over the sale of illegal drugs.

- Swingley had told Al Hirst on the night of the killings that he had already killed two people that night and, holding a gun to Hirst's head, threatened to "blow [his] brains out," according to people who knew Hirst and had heard the story firsthand from him.

- Swingley had gone to Florida following the Westside Park killings, even though he apparently didn't know anyone there, and he ended up living under a highway bridge. While there, he got in trouble with the law for holding a knife to the throat of a man who had said Swingley "didn't have the balls" to leave the country to go to Australia.

- People close to Swingley, including his mother, had heard rumors that he had killed the teens in the park.

- Swingley had told an associate he went to Westside Park that night to sell cocaine.

Marianne Vorhees, the judge of Delaware Circuit Court 1, approved and signed the DNA warrant on November 14, 2018.

On November 20, 2018, Sloan and another Muncie police detective made the trip to the state prison outside Terre Haute, across the Hoosier state from Muncie. Sloan expected that Swingley would again tell him to "fuck off," as he had done in April 2012. Instead, when Sloan explained that he had a court-ordered warrant to collect some of the inmate's DNA, Swingley not only agreed to give the DNA sample through the application of a swab in his mouth, but he also sat down for a forty-minute interview.

Swingley—his skin covered with tattoos to the top of his neck, just below his chin—responded to Sloan's question about the murders of Dixon and Dowell by saying that the police detective had the wrong man. He said that not only had he not killed the teens but it was his understanding that Kimberly's stepfather had committed the crime.

At the end of interview, Sloan left and returned to Muncie with a DNA sample but nothing else.

COLD CASES AS ENTERTAINMENT

I f you thought Pinterest was a website where people could post pictures of their favorite recipes or home décor, you might have found it odd to come across a photograph of Ethan Dixon and Kimberly Dowell standing next to Ethan's Volkswagen Rabbit hatchback, a snapshot taken in the days leading up to their shooting deaths in Westside Park. The photograph was taken from an article in the *Star Press* newspaper that was written by the authors of this book and loaned to the authors by Kimberly's father, Anthony Dowell. The pinned photograph of the happy teenagers posing next to the car in which their lives would soon end is a jarring reminder of how much of society considers cold cases and unsolved murders entertainment.

The Pinterest photograph comes from a website that specializes in reprinting true crime stories from around the country, sometimes with joking headlines. The website itself linked the image to the *Star Press* articles about the Westside Park murders.

When did true crime and cold cases and unsolved murders become fodder for popular entertainment? It would be impossible to say, but stories of murder and mayhem have always been told and retold, from the Bible and dime novels of Old West lawmen and outlaws to Truman Capote's groundbreaking 1965 "nonfiction novel" *In Cold Blood* and Ann Rule's true crime books like *The Stranger Beside Me*, her 1980 book about her unwitting friendship with serial killer Ted Bundy.

Newspapers, the training ground and lifelong vocation of the authors of this book, have more than capitalized on true crime stories over the years.

For decades, newspapers recounting tragic deaths and grisly murders walked a fine line between "just the facts" retellings and sensational accounts.

But nothing made true crime boom quite like the Internet. Websites featuring tales of murder and unsolved crimes number beyond counting. Some are scholarly, like *True Crime Diary*, which was created by author Michelle McNamara. She stumbled across stories of true crime in online forums and found the Internet as a way for sleuths—both professional and amateur and unpaid—to compare notes on unsolved crimes that had sometimes fallen off the radar of the public and been covered up on the desks of police detectives by the files of other crimes that were also deserving of resolution.

McNamara won the trust of active and retired police investigators throughout southern California and slowly began to link a series of murders, rapes and home invasions together as the work of a criminal she dubbed the "Golden State Killer." McNamara's book was published in 2018, following her early and tragic death of natural causes, and police, using DNA information submitted to an ancestry website, arrested a man they said they believed was responsible for many of the crimes.

In the case of the Golden State Killer, years of research and shared information online, as well as the work of McNamara, kept the case on the front burner. While many of the crimes were cold cases, public interest kept the case from growing truly cold.

It's hard to equate McNamara's work with other online obsessions with cold cases, including YouTube videos of a man who, in one instance, looks to one side of the camera and reads, from a computer screen, one of the Westside Park articles by the authors of this book. The man's viewers praise his efforts in the comments on the video.

Along with television shows like *Unsolved Mysteries*, which features host Robert Stack and a series of cold cases from 1987 to 2010, network and cable channel shows have recounted hundreds and thousands of true crime stories. Some police jurisdictions have not only cooperated but also sought out the attention of these shows.

More recently, the rise of podcasts—audio recordings, some barebones and some with high production values, available for download on phones so true crime "fans" can take their "favorite" murders with them—has provided a fertile ground for true crime stories. The podcasts, including some featuring a breathy host who encourages the predominately female audience to settle in with the story and a bottle of wine, have become one of the most successful forms of true crime storytelling.

Some podcasts stem from hours of research and interviews, while others simply retread newspaper stories from recent decades, sometimes without attribution to the writers and reporters at newspapers and TV stations who originally brought the cold cases back into the light. One popular podcast pulled some episodes from its lineup after being called out for what appeared to be plagiarism, or copying the work of established news sources. Some of the podcasts are more sophisticated than the man on camera reading a newspaper article line by line from his computer monitor—and some are not.

While some true crime storytelling is aimed at an audience seeking "chills"—an audience that might consider buying not only a book but also a mail-order mattress or cellphone plan—some is intended to enlighten its audience and, with a stroke of luck, prompt answers to longstanding mysteries and maybe even bring justice to people whose deaths were forgotten by everyone but their still-grieving survivors and, in some cases, a handful of police investigators.

The survivors and cops would like nothing better than to put a name to a faceless killer and close the file on a long-ago murder.

JUSTICE DELAYED

The test performed on the sample of James "Jimmy" Swingley's DNA taken during Muncie police investigator Nathan Sloan's visit to the Wabash Valley Correctional Facility on November 20, 2018, did not provide a conclusive match linking Swingley to what is perhaps the only piece of evidence belonging to the killer of Ethan Dixon and Kimberly Dowell: the gun holster that was found in Dixon's car.

Potential DNA evidence on the holster had been damaged and muddied since 1985.

Sloan has not wavered in his belief that Swingley is the strongest person of interest in the murders of Dowell and Dixon. Sloan cites the lie detector test in 1987, during which Swingley failed on "all of the pertinent questions about Westside Park." Sloan also cites the "trail" of people who later told police that Swingley had told them he had killed the two teenagers in the park that night. "Out of all the persons of interest in the case, he's definitely the best one," Sloan said of Swingley.

Marvin Campbell, the longtime police investigator and former deputy chief of the Muncie Police Department who had focused his investigation on Kimberly Dowell's stepfather, scoffs at Sloan's focus on Swingley. "Nobody brags about killing somebody," Campbell said. "Unless [current investigators] can answer questions like what he did with the gun, they don't have it. If they had any real good evidence, you think he'd be charged by now," Campbell said.

Sloan said he hoped that this book could bring about some resolution to the longstanding cold case. "I hope this book sparks new leads," Sloan said. "Maybe someone will come forward with information." Sloan, the chief of police in Muncie starting on January 1, 2020, asked that anyone with information about the case contact him via email at nsloan@cityofmuncie.com.

Swingley, who is still serving his sixty-five-year prison sentence for killing Brian Insco, maintained his silence when he was contacted and asked to provide comments for this book.

In October 2019, the authors wrote to Swingley at the Wabash Valley Correctional Facility in Carlisle, Indiana, near the Illinois state line. In the letter, the authors asked Swingley just four questions:

- Did he murder Ethan Dixon and Kimberly Dowell?

- If he did not, why did he tell friends that he had?

- If he did not, does he know who did?

- What was his reaction to the Muncie Police Department's efforts to tie him to the killings of Dixon and Dowell?

The authors included a self-addressed, stamped envelope for Swingley to reply if he wanted. At the time the writing of this book was completed, more than five months later, Swingley had not responded to the letter.

Acccording to the Indiana Department of Correction, Swingley is due to be released from prison on July 10, 2030, when he is sixty-seven years old.

In 2030, Kimberly Dowell would have been sixty years old and Ethan Dixon would have been sixty-one years old.

46

"WHAT WERE THEY THINKING ABOUT?"

Thirty-five years after the killings of Kimberly Dowell and Ethan Dixon in Westside Park, Muncie—like a lot of cities in the American Midwest—was trying to cope with its present while acknowledging its past and hoping to determine its future.

In 1985, Muncie's status as an industrial powerhouse, where thousands of men and women went to work in factories every day, was slowly coming to an end. In a little more than two decades, the largest of the auto parts plants that had once sparked the city's economic engine were closed. Muncie's Chevrolet and BorgWarner Automotive Plants followed factories like Ball Brothers, American Lawnmower and Delco out of the city. Although some manufacturing remained, it was on a much smaller scale than the factories of old. The city's economy shifted to healthcare, education, retail and similar service industries. Many thousands moved out of the city, looking for jobs or just a better way of life.

The loss of jobs, the loss of population and the loss of lives to drug abuse (as Muncie became known for first cocaine use then methamphetamine and prescription painkiller abuse) took a greater toll than lives lost to sudden violence.

As some people left Muncie for the promise of jobs elsewhere and school enrollment fell, Northside High School's doors were closed in 1988. Other schools followed, leaving the city with a single high school and a handful of elementary and middle schools that continued to struggle financially.

Failed revitalization efforts and outright schemes dogged the city far into the twenty-first century, with dreamer followed by wishful thinker followed by scam artist all promised to create jobs and restore Muncie to whatever glory it had achieved in the past.

Muncie residents couldn't turn to their elected leaders for guidance, as the political corruption that had always been part of the community and which had helped it earn the nickname "Little Chicago" became more blatant. For several years leading up to the thirty-fifth anniversary of the Westside Park murders, the city's government, as run by the latest in a long line of political party regulars, was under investigation by federal authorities, resulting in FBI raids of government offices and criminal charges filed against some of the elected and appointed officials by the Department of Justice.

If Muncie ever had any innocence to lose—because we've seen that the city has always been a rough-and-tumble place, home to a hard-living workforce, political chicanery, random acts of violence and corruption—did the city lose that innocence when two teenagers, still children really, were shot to death in Westside Park?

In the fall of 2019, fallen leaves marked the spot in Muncie's Westside Park where Ethan Dixon and Kimberly Dowell were killed in 1985. *Courtesy of Jordan Kartholl.*

Whether its innocence was lost or not, Westside Park remains. How many who bike or walk along its trail, who watch as their children or grandchildren enjoy its playground or just drive past along White River Boulevard, think of the murders of Kimberly Dowell and Ethan Dixon?

Julie Davey, Ethan's friend, who didn't succeed in persuading him to skip school with her the day before he was killed, has spent little time in Muncie as an adult. Once, when she was in the city, the park was a stark reminder of what she, her classmates, her school and the city of Muncie lost on September 28, 1985. The visit prompted her to think about what her schoolmates were thinking about, talking about, on that fall evening. "Fifteen years ago, my daughter had a soccer tournament in Muncie," she recalled.

> *Her coach didn't know the story, and we took a break at Westside Park. I said a prayer, and my daughter asked what I was doing. I didn't know what to say. What were they thinking about those last few minutes? Back in high school, I sometimes drove a car with a moon roof, and I remember just lying back and looking up at the stars. Is that what they were doing? Were they having a deep discussion? What was on their minds?*

BIBLIOGRAPHY

Chapter 1

Anonymous. "September 1985 Entertainment Options in Muncie–Advertisements in the *Muncie Star*." *Muncie Star*, September 1985.
Davey, Julie. Interview with the authors. 2019.
Leffingwell, Amy. Interview with the authors. 2019.
Swingley, James "Jimmy" (false name in police traffic stop). Comments about killing two people. Interview with Nathan Sloan of the Muncie Police Department. 2019.
——. Court records for resulting traffic-related charges against Swingley. Interview with Nathan Sloan of the Muncie Police Department. 2019.

Chapter 2

Campbell, Marvin. The crime scene. Interview with the authors. Also *Muncie Star*, September 29, 1985, and September 30, 1985.
Winkle, Joe. Arrival. Interview with the authors. 2019.
Winters, Terry. Recollections. Interview with the authors. *Star Press*, 2014.

Chapter 3

Davey, Julie. Interview with the authors. 2019.
Leffingwell, Amy. Interview with the authors. 2019.
McDonald, Dan. Interview with the authors. 2019.
Multiple articles from the *Muncie Star*, September 29, 1985, and September 30, 1985.
Rankin, Kay. Interview with the authors. 2019.

Chapter 4

Canan, Joe. Glenn Scroggins anecdote. *Muncie Evening Press*, December 1986.
Final autopsy report for Ethan Dixon, September 29, 1985, Indiana State Board of Health, coroner's certificate of death for Ethan Dixon, report of radiologic consultation for Ethan Dixon, Delaware County Emergency Medical Service medication and treatment record for Ethan Dixon, September 28, 1985, coroner's verdict issued by Delaware County coroner Glenn Scroggins on October 21, 1985.
Final autopsy report for Kimberly Dowell, September 29, 1985, report of radiologic consultation for Kimberly Dowell, Delaware County Emergency Medical Service medication and treatment record for Kimberly Dowell, September 28, 1985, coroner's verdict issued by Delaware County coroner Glenn Scroggins on October 21, 1985.

Chapter 5

Campbell, Marvin. Interview with the authors. 2019.
Hermansen, Vicki. "Authorities Seek Motive in Slaying of Two Teenagers." *Muncie Star*, September 30, 1985.
Newlin, Diana. "Probe Centers on Two Cars." *Muncie Star*, October 3, 1985.
———. "Slayings Might Involve 3, Police Say." *Muncie Star*, October 1, 1985.

Chapter 6

Davey, Julie. Interview with the authors. 2019.

Leffingwell, Amy. Interview with the authors. 2019.

Rankin, Kay. Interview with the authors. 2019.

Chapter 7

Anonymous. "Girl, 8, Hit by Car Dies." *Muncie Star* and *Muncie Evening Press*, June 10, 1972.

Multiple articles about the death of Jack D. Swingley in the *Muncie Star* and the *Muncie Evening Press*, January 28, 29, 30 and 31, 1981.

Sloan, Nathan. Comments in police interview of Desiree Dawn. Interview with the authors. 2019.

Chapter 8

Campbell, Marvin. Interview with the authors. 2019.

Metzger, Juli North. "Status of Case, New Sources." *Muncie Star*, Sunday, October 6, 1985.

Multiple articles about the deaths of Carol Revis and Wendi Matson in the *Muncie Star* and the *Muncie Evening Press*, December 6, 7, 8 and 29, 1985.

Chapter 9

Campbell, Marvin. Identification of suspect in sketch as James "Jimmy" Swingley. Interview by the authors. 2019.

Davey, Julie. Interview with the authors. 2019.

Drawing of Westside Park the night of the murders, uncredited, in the *Muncie Evening Press*, October 8, 1985.

Leffingwell, Amy. Interview with the authors. 2019.

Multiple articles about Muncie, Indiana, in the days and weeks following the Westside Park murders in the *Muncie Star* and *Muncie Evening Press*.

Rankin, Kay. Interview with the authors. 2019.

Sketch of suspect by an uncredited police department sketch artist in the *Muncie Evening Press*, October 7, 1985.

Sloan, Nathan. James "Jimmy" Swingley in Florida in 1985. Interview with the authors, 2019.

Chapter 10

Multiple articles about 1985 news events in the *Muncie Star* and the *Muncie Evening Press*, January through December 1985.

Muncie history as "Little Chicago" by the authors.

Muncie history by the authors.

Muncie population numbers, 1940, 1950, 1980, 2019, U.S. Census.

Walker, Douglas, and Keith Roysdon. *Muncie Murder & Mayhem*. Charleston, SC: The History Press, 2018.

———. *Wicked Muncie*. Charleston, SC: The History Press, 2016.

Chapter 11

Davey, Julie. Interview with the authors. 2019.

Leffingwell, Amy. Interview with the authors. 2019.

Loy, Bob. "Northside High School to Be Dedicated." *Muncie Evening Press*, December 3, 1970.

Multiple articles about school history in the *Muncie Star* and the *Muncie Evening Press*, 1965 through 1988.

Multiple articles about the closing of Northside High School in the *Muncie Star* and the *Muncie Evening Press*, June 7–8, 1988.

Rankin, Kay. Interview with the authors. 2019.

Chapter 12

Anonymous. "Nancy Vogelgesang Death." *Muncie Evening Press*, December 26, 1987.

Rankin, Kay. Interview with the authors. 2019.

Sloan, Nathan. Interview with the authors. 2019.

Vogelgesang, Donald. Interview with the authors. *Star Press*, September 29, 1997.

Chapter 13

Multiple advertisements and articles in the *Muncie Star* and the *Muncie Evening Press*, September 1985.

Multiple articles about Madison Street cruising by teens in the *Muncie Star* and the *Muncie Evening Press*, including one from April 26, 1980.

Chapter 14

Black, Jim. "Off Limits Rule Aimed at Thieves, Not Fishermen." *Muncie Star*, July 23, 1972.

Multiple articles about alternatives to teenagers cruising Madison Street in the *Muncie Star* and the *Muncie Evening Press*, including one from April 26, 1980.

Multiple articles about fighting and rape in the *Muncie Star* and the *Muncie Evening Press*.

Penticuff, David. "Watchers Seek 'Fuzzball' in the Sky." *Muncie Star*, April 30, 1986.

Usher, Brian. "Patriots Observe Centennial." *Muncie Star*, July 5, 1965.

Wilham, T.J. "Woman's Body Found in Prairie Creek Lake." *Muncie Star*, September 12, 1999.

Chapter 15

Anonymous. "Muncie Mall Tenant Lineup." In *Polks City Directory*. Detroit, MI: R.L. Polk and Co., 1985.

Chapter 16

Charges filed, including no operator's license in possession. Delaware County Superior Court 4 records, case filed November 26, 1986.

Default judgment issued. Delaware County Superior Court 4 records, various, 1991.

Goldsmith, Greg. "Police Rounding Up 12 Here Indicted as Racketeers." *Muncie Evening Press* and *Muncie Star*, March 8, 1985.

Jackson, William. "Racketeering Charge Dropped." *Muncie Star*, September 10, 1985.

Chapter 17

Armed and Famous. Aired on CBS, January 2007.

Davis, Peter, and Tom Cohen, executive producers. *Middletown.* Aired on PBS, 1982.

Love, Nancy. "*NY Times* Reporter Finds 'Middletown' Rings True," *Muncie Star* and *Muncie Evening Press*, December 8 and 9, 1970.

Lynd, Robert, and Helen Lynd. *Middletown: A Study in Modern American Culture.* New York: Columbia University, 1929.

———. *Middletown in Transition.* New York: Columbia University, 1937.

Movies and TV shows mentioning Muncie and various pop culture references, cited in text.

Multiple articles about the Middletown studies in the *Muncie Star*, April 1937.

Chapter 18

Davis, Peter, and Tom Cohen, executive producers. *Middletown.* "The Campaign," James P. Carey versus Alan Wilson election. Aired on PBS, 1982.

Walker, Douglas, and Keith Roysdon. "Mayor James P. Carey History." *Star Press*, October 17, 2006.

Chapter 19

Anonymous. "Balloon Ascensions." *Muncie Daily Times*, June 5, 1894.

———. "'Burly' Tramp." *Muncie Daily Herald*, June 14, 1895.

———. "Warm Afternoons." *Muncie Morning News*, May 18, 1894.

———. "Westside Park Here to Be Revived." *Muncie Star*, July 8, 1953.

———. "Westside Park Naked People, Rape." *Muncie Star*, June 23, 1983.

———. "Westside Park Poem, P.D.Q." *Muncie Morning Star*, December 11, 1931.

Ferris, Jack. "Foundations of Old Amusement Ride Found at Westside Park." *Muncie Star*, July 30, 1961.

Multiple articles about the indoor skating rink, 1899 to 1908.

Chapter 20

Anonymous. "Lovers Lane Murders." *Weekly World News*, November 12, 1985.

David Berkowitz, "Son of Sam." Multiple sources, including "Mr. Nice Guy Stuns Neighbors." *Rutland Daily Herald*, August 14, 1977.

Drexler, Paul. "Ultimate Puzzle: The World of Zodiology," *San Francisco Examiner*, August 16, 2015.

Multiple sources from Gale Patrick Irish, including an article from the *San Bernardino County Sun*, March 22, 1963.

Multiple sources from Ralph Lobaugh, including an article from the *Noblesville Ledger*, July 27, 1977.

Multiple sources related to the Zodiac killings.

Pierce, Charles B., dir. *The Town that Dreaded Sundown*. Los Angeles: American International Pictures, 1976.

Chapter 21

Campbell, Marvin. Interview with the authors. 2019.

Killings of Shaun Champlin and Tina Montoy in Concordia, Kansas, *Salina* (KS) *Journal*, October 20, 1980.

Manning, Carl. "Still a Mystery." *Salina* (Kansas) *Journal*, April 26, 2003.

Walker, Douglas, and Keith Roysdon. "Connection Between Westside Park Killings and Champlin and Montoy Killings in Kansas." *Star Press*, September 19, 2010.

Chapter 22

Leffingwell, Amy. Interview with authors. 2019.

Sloan, Nathan. "Other 'Suspects' Reported to Police." Interview with the authors. 2019.

Chapter 23

Anonymous. "Coroner's Inquiry into Westside Park Slayings Is Sought." *Muncie Evening Press*, January 27, 1986.

———. "Own Gun Kills Youth in Hunting Accident." *Muncie Star*, December 15, 1986.

Canan, Joe. "Coroner Won't Call Inquiry into Slayings in Westside Park," *Muncie Evening Press*, January 30, 1986.

———. "Joint City–County Homicide Investigation to Be Revived." *Muncie Evening Press*, December 18, 1986.

Davis, Ervin. "Letter to the Editor About Thomas Dunlap." *Muncie Star*, December 19, 1986.

Chapter 24

Davey, Julie. Interview with authors. 2019.

Multiple articles about the death of Gregg Winters, December 1990 to present.

Walker, Douglas, and Keith Roysdon. "Terry Winters Recalls Westside Park Slayings." *Star Press*, September 21, 2014.

Chapter 25

Campbell, Marvin. Interview with authors. 2019.

Walker, Douglas, and Keith Roysdon. "Tenth Anniversary Stakeout Recounted by Robert Weller." *Star Press*, September 19, 2010.

———. "Vogelgesang Interview with Attorney Charles 'Chic' Clark." *Star Press*, September 28, 1997.

———. "The Westside Park Murders 25 Years Later." *Star Press*, September 19, 2010.

Chapter 26

Sloan, Nathan. Renewed interviews, old and new leads. Interview with the authors. 2019.

Chapter 27

Multiple articles on the killings of "The Railroad Killer," including one from the *Fort Worth Star-Telegram*, 1999 and 2000.

Sloan, Nathan. Lead on Ángel Maturino Reséndiz, also known as "The Railroad Killer" or "The Railway Killer." Interview with the authors. 2019.

Chapter 28

Sloan, Nathan. Nathan Sloan and other investigators following up on other credible Leads, interview with the authors. 2019.

Chapter 29

Sloan, Nathan. Activities of small group of associates, interview with the authors. 2019.

Chapter 30

Banks, Deborah. "Murder of Brian Insco." *Muncie Star*, November 13, 1996.
Sloan, Nathan. Reports of witnesses and informants. Interview with authors. 2019.
Walker, Douglas. "Delaware County Grand Jury Indicts James 'Jimmy' Swingley for Murder of Brian Insco." *Star Press*, May 23, 1998.
———. "James 'Jimmy' Swingley Found Guilty of Murder in Brian Insco Death." *Star Press*, February 19, 1999.
———. "James 'Jimmy' Swingley Sentenced to 65 Years for Murder of Brian Insco." *Star Press*, April 9, 1999.
———. "You Could Get Away with Murder in Delaware County." *Star Press*, February 19, 1999.

Chapter 31

Anonymous. "Local Killer Dead." *Star Press*, August 2, 2007.
Canan, Joe. "Death of Howard 'Pete' Journay." *Muncie Evening Press*, May 9, 1979.
Hardin, Mary. "Police Find No New Clues in Brutal Double Murder." *Muncie Star* and *Muncie Evening Press*, May 10, 1980.

Multiple articles on the deaths of Russell Krull, David Grimes and Raymond Waldo in the *Muncie Star* and the *Muncie Evening Press* on various dates in May and June 1980.

Pitts, Eldon. "Second Rail Crossing Death Within a Week." *Star Press*, February 9, 1979.

Reed, Richard. Inundated with homicides. Interview with the authors. 2019.

Roysdon, Keith, and Douglas Walker. "Howard 'Pete' Journay Article in Cold Case Muncie." *Star Press*, December 2, 2012.

Chapter 32

Maynard, Greg. "All But 16 Of 160 Murders Solved." *Muncie Star*, June 4, 1989.

Walker, Douglas, and Keith Roysdon. "Murder of Maggie Mae Fleming, Cold Case: Muncie." *Star Press*, November 27, 2011.

———. "Murder of William Gump, Cold Case: Muncie." *Star Press*, November 27, 2011.

Chapter 33

Walker, Douglas, and Keith Roysdon. "Cold Case: Muncie on Sam Drummer." *Star Press*, June 2, 2013.

Chapter 34

Sloan, Nathan. James "Jimmy" Swingley becomes focus of Nathan Sloan's investigation; results of lie detector test; account of Albert Hirst; Sloan attempted interview with Swingley in prison. Interview with the authors. 2019.

Chapter 35

Sloan, Nathan. Desiree Dawn, mother of James "Jimmy" Swingley, February 2014 interview with Nathan Sloan. Interview with the authors. 2019.

————. Interview with Delaware County Jail employee "Edith Evans," in August 2013. Interview with the authors. 2019.

————. September 2018 interview with "Mark Mason," "Fucking Jimmy Swingley." Interview with the authors. 2019.

Chapter 36

Dixon, Steve. "Letter to Muncie Police Department." April 19, 2002.

————. Personal communications with the authors. 2019.

Sloan, Nathan. Dixon 2013 comments to Nathan Sloan, Interview with the authors. 2019.

————. Vogelgesang 2013 comments to Nathan Sloan, Interview with the authors. 2019.

Vogelgesang, Donald . Personal communications with the authors. 2019.

Chapter 37

Dowell, Dr. Anthony. Interview with the authors. 2019.

Chapter 38

Dowell, Dr. Anthony. Interview with the authors. 2019.

Chapter 39

Death of Michael J. "Mick" Alexander, Walker, Douglas and Roysdon, Keith, *Walker/Roysdon Report*, June 18, 2017.

Michael J. "Mick" Alexander obituary, uncredited, *Star Press*, June 17, 2017.

Reed, Richard. Interview with authors. 2019.

Chapter 40

Canan, Joe. "Formation of City–County Homicide Team." *Muncie Evening Press*, January 7, 1980.

———. "Reforming of City–County Homicide Team." *Muncie Evening Press*, December 18, 1986.

Gary Carmichael comment of "childish stuff led to disbanding of homicide team" in the *Muncie Star*, November 1, 1981.

Jackson, William. "Hypno Investigators." *Muncie Star*, December 27, 1981.

———. "Muncie Forms its Own Homicide Team." *Muncie Star*, October 16, 1981.

Stodghill, Dick. "Own Homicide Team Has a Hard Act to Follow." *Muncie Evening Press*, October 29, 1981.

Chapter 41

Cook, Jerry. Interview with the authors. 2019.

Heath, Richard. Interview with the authors. 2019.

Chapter 42

Court documents in Brian Insco murder case file, including text of James "Jimmy" Swingley's filings to the Indiana Court of Appeals.

Chapter 43

Details from probable cause documents issued November 14, 2018, from Delaware Circuit Court 1 for a body warrant to obtain DNA from James "Jimmy" Swingley.

Sloan, Nathan. Interviews with the authors. 2019 and 2020.

Chapter 44

Capote, Truman. *In Cold Blood*. New York: Penguin Random House, 1965.

McNamara, Michelle. *I'll Be Gone in the Dark*. New York: HarperCollins, 2018.

———. *True Crime Diary*. www.truecrimediary.com.

Rule, Ann. *The Stranger Beside Me*. New York: W.W. Norton & Co., 1980

Chapter 45

Campbell, Marvin. Interview with the authors. 2019.
Sloan, Nathan. Interview with the authors. 2020.

Chapter 46

Davey, Julie. Interview with the authors. 2019.

INDEX

ABOUT THE AUTHORS

Keith Roysdon is a lifelong writer and journalist. For more than forty years, starting when he was in high school, he worked in the newspaper industry in Indiana, where he was a reporter, columnist, reviewer and editor. His stories prompted and revealed local, state and federal investigations of corruption and wrongdoing on the part of officials. He has won more than two dozen state journalism awards and two national journalism awards, some of those for work with his writing partner Douglas Walker. Their work includes dozens of articles about cold cases, or unsolved murders. The two won the 2018 Indiana Society for Professional Journalists Award for best nonfiction book for their *Muncie Murder & Mayhem* true crime book. The two also wrote *Wicked Muncie*. Both books are available from Arcadia and The History Press. Roysdon, who also writes fiction, is married to his wife, Robin, and has a son, James.

Veteran journalist Douglas Walker has covered the criminal justice system in east-central Indiana for most of the past three decades. For more than a quarter of a century, he has served in reporting and editing roles for the *Star Press* and its predecessor, the *Muncie Evening Press*. Walker has received dozens of awards for writing, reporting and public service from state, regional and national journalism organizations. Many have been the result of his collaboration with Keith Roysdon, including, through 2018, a long-running weekly column about politics. The Ball State University graduate is an eighth-generation resident of the Muncie, Indiana area.

Through his reporting, Walker has taken his readers to hundreds of crime scenes, scores of murder trials, two presidential inaugurations, more than thirty election nights and even into the death chamber at the Indiana State Prison for an eyewitness account of an execution. He is married to his wife, Jennifer, and has three children and four grandchildren.